Starting to Manage:
the essential skills

Gerard M Blair

 Chartwell Bratt

 Studentlitteratur

British Library Cataloguing in Publication Data
A catalogue record for this book is available from the British Library

All rights reserved. No part of this publication may be reproduced or
transmitted in any form or by any means, electronic or mechanical,
including photocopying, recording, or any information storage and retrieval system,
without permission in writing from the publisher.

© Gerard M Blair and Chartwell-Bratt 1993.

Chartwell-Bratt (Publishing and Training) Ltd
ISBN 0-86238-336-6

Printed in Sweden
Studentlitteratur, Lund
ISBN 91-44-39441-1

| Printing | 1 2 3 4 5 6 7 8 9 10 | 1998 97 96 95 94 93 |

*For Amy, Eccup, Thump
and the Alien*

About the Author

Gerard M Blair has an MA in Mathematics, a Diploma in Computer Science, and a PhD in Electrical Engineering; and is an Associate Member of the Institution of Electrical Engineers. After gaining his doctorate in microchip design, he worked in industry rising to Project Leader with European Silicon Structures (ES2) while enduring a two-hour commute. This enabled him to read widely and so to indulge his interest in Management Skill development. He now lectures in Project Management and VLSI Design at the University of Edinburgh.

He welcomes feedback at: Department of Electrical Engineering, The University of Edinburgh, The King's Buildings, Edinburgh EH9 3JL, Scotland UK; by phone: (+31) 650 5592; by fax: (+31) 650 6554; or on email: gerard@ee.ed.ac.uk.

Preface

The subject of this book is the skills which are needed for the management of small teams and small projects: the skills of communication, leadership and organization. These are used by managers in every industry to coordinate and direct the activity of their teams. These are the skills in which no one ever thinks to train a manager until long after they are first needed.

The idea of the book was born from personal frustration. I entered industry technically competent, but very quickly I needed to perform management functions for which I had neither experience nor training. The demands were not particularly difficult except in that they were totally different from anything I had encountered before. The expectation (common in industry) was that I would learn 'to manage' either by magic or by osmosis. What I needed was a book on how to start, how to look after a small team of staff, how to communicate upwards and get things done below.

In fact, I read widely – helped by a long commute on British Rail. When I left the company after three years, I had specified and developed my own product ideas, recruited and managed a small team, and been given responsibility for the quality of a large portion of the company's output. This book is the skill-set I needed in these three years. This is the book I wish I had read first.

The book is based upon a course given to a group of electrical engineers during the final two years of a Masters degree at Edinburgh University. The aim of the course is to provide these students with sufficient management skills to enable them to assume a level of responsibility commensurate with their technical skills. The content of the course was derived from a survey of first-time employers of previous graduates. Thus the *essential* skills are those requested by employers: the skills they need in their junior managers.

My thanks go to the large number of organizations who have provided help, material and encouragement. European Silicon Structures (ES2) provided the initial environment and opportunity for learning. The University of Edinburgh Enterprise Centre provided funds and many industrial contacts. Three companies provided places for me on their in-house training courses: Royal Bank of Scotland, Hewlett-Packard, and Standard Life Assurance. British Telecom ran (and left behind the material for) a training course for my students. Staff from IBM and ScotRail have provided lectures. The Association of Project Managers encouraged and published the initial skills survey in their journal, *Project*. The Institution of Electrical Engineers published my series of ten two-monthly articles on management skills, upon which this book is based, in the *IEE Engineering Management Journal*. My thanks also go to the MEng students without whom none of this would have been possible, and to Amy Blair for providing a sanity check on my writing and ideas.

CONTENTS

To Begin at the Beginning	1
The Beginning	2
What YOU can do	4
Images of a Manager	5
A General Approach	7
Management Skills	9
To Begin	11
Formal Presentations	13
Why Bother?	14
The Plan	16
Structure	18
The Beginning	21
The Ending	22
Visual Aids	23
The Delivery	24
The Techniques of Speech	27
The Actual Mechanics	31
Constant Learning	35
Team Work	37
Why a Group?	38
Group Roles	39
Group Development	42
Group Skills	44
Putting this into Practice	50
Time Management	53
Watch the Time	54
Waste Disposal	56
Doing the Work of Others	57
External Appointments	59
Scheduling Work	60
Looking Further Afield	62
A Parenthesis on Stress	63
A Total Review	65
The Written Word	68
Management Writing	69
Initial Planning	71
Draft, Revise and Edit	73
Getting Started	79
A Small Assignment	80
The Gentle Art of Delegation	85
Planning to Delegate	86
Support and Monitoring	89
Outcomes and Failure	92
Making Time	94
To Capture Quality	96
What is 'Quality'?	97
Team Quality	101
Quality for the Future	108
Conversation Management	111
Ambiguity Avoidance	112
Practical Points	114
Telephony or Cacophony?	117
The Selection Interview	119
Meeting Management (I)	121
Meeting Management (II)	123
Communication	127
People	129
Behaviour	130
Motivation	130
People Problems	134
Where to Seek Solutions	138
A Little Practice	139
A Manager of the People	144
Planning a Project	146
Project Management	147
The Specification	147
Providing Structure	150
Establishing Controls	156
The Artistry in Planning	158
Planning for the Future	163
A Great Manager	166
The Main Theme	166
Starting a Revolution	168
Vision	169
Prescience	171
Changes of Focus	173
Flexibility	174
The Leaders	176

Chapter: 1
To Begin at the Beginning

Work was like cats were supposed to be: if you disliked and feared it and tried to keep out of its way, it knew at once and sought you out and jumped on your lap and climbed all over you to show how much it loved you
(Kingsley Amis)

This is a book for the surprised manager. This is a book for all the people who one day woke up and faced promotion (whoopee!) to a post which meant taking responsibility (oh?) for projects and people. This is a book for all of you who were never told what promotion means.

Many books on management deal with how to turn whole corporations from declining dodos into energetic eagles (or vicious vultures). This is not one of those books. This is about YOU. This is not here to promote a new era of industrial strength and international dominance, this is here to promote you. This is about what you can do for yourself and for your group.

The good news is that the first steps to becoming a really *great* manager are simply common sense. Most of the problems you face have simple solutions. If someone were to pose such a problem to you, you would be able to give them a good answer. But would you have thought to ask the question yourself? If you were sitting comfortably at home and you heard about some daft novice who did such-and-such at the first team meeting, you could probably laugh just as loud as a company Director. But if you had actually been there, if you had not seen or thought about the problem before, if you had had to make a fast decision – you too might have done the same, or worse. The difficulty with common sense is that it is not very common, and it has to be acquired.

1.1 The Beginning

There are two major problems when you start to manage:

- you do not actually think about management issues because you do not recognize them
- you have only a limited experience upon which to draw to create solutions

Put simply, things normally go wrong not because you are stupid but only because you have never thought about it before. This is the book which outlines the problems that all new managers have to face; this is the book which suggests solutions for you to consider; you are the person who decides. In the leisure of your own armchair, you will think about issues without pressure and learn from what others have thought before you. Then, when a management problem occurs at work, you will have already thought about something similar – and you will be able to apply your common sense.

Management is a skill – and like any other skill it comes with experience and practice. If you think that is not true, ask the better athletes or musicians how long they practise in a day. Your experience, however, will be made far more beneficial in developing that skill if you prepare for the experience and if you deliberately exploit it. Thus tennis players do not simply play tennis, they determine their own strengths, they work to overcome their weaknesses, they think carefully about what they do and how to improve, and they listen to what their trainer suggests. Many people have managed before you, and many people have succeeded. Often they know what they did right – they can tell you what it was.

Consider a simple skill like driving a car. When you were a child, you often saw grown-ups driving. You sat beside them, you watched the feet moving, sometimes you even held the wheel (before you knew this was illegal). So, was that enough to teach you how to drive? Could you have simply slipped into the driving seat and taken over? Would you have driven a racing car around a Grand-Prix track on your first afternoon? Of course not, someone had to show you how. That is not to say you watched someone do it; someone actually sat down beside you in the passenger seat (trying not to look frightened) and helped you to acquire that skill.

When master craftsmen took on an apprentice, they did not simply point to the materials and say: 'Get on with it'; they showed the apprentice the skills in simple steps and then said: 'Practise'. Yet a common experience at work is that new managers are expected to absorb their skills from thin air, by some magical form of osmosis. There is the irrational belief that people will develop management skills simply by being called names like: manager, supervisor, project leader. One day you are a gofer, the next you have gofers to go for you; yet the newly-appointed manager receives virtually no training. Managers are meant to 'feel their way', to 'jump-in at the deep end', to 'go where many have gone before – without bothering anyone else', and the results are not surprising.

There is a theory (known as the Peter Principle) that people rise to the level of their own incompetence, in that they get promoted until they no longer do the job well – and then stay there, performing badly for the rest of their working lives. This is probably true because most organizations actually ignore the difference between the technical competence by which the lower levels impress their superiors and the managerial skills which are needed in the higher levels. This problem can only be addressed by training – but if you are in the Peter trap already then you will have to train yourself.

Let us summarize: management is about pausing to ask yourself the right questions so that your common sense can provide the answers. By thinking explicitly about your management skills, by deliberately practising and striving to improve, by learning from the experience and suggestions of previous managers, you can develop your own common-sense approach to management practice.

1.2 What YOU can do

When you gain managerial responsibility, your first option is the easy option: do what is expected of you. You are new at the job, so people will understand. You can learn (slowly) by your mistakes and probably you will try to devote as much time as possible to the rest of your work (which is what your were good at anyway). Those extra little 'management' problems are just common sense, so try to deal with them as they come up.

Your second option is far more exciting: find an empty telephone box, put on a cape and bright-red underpants, and become a SuperManager.

When you become a manager, you gain control over your own work; not all of it, but some of it. You can change things. You can do things differently. You actually have the authority to make a huge impact upon the way in which your staff work and how they (and you) are perceived by the rest of the company. You can define your own work environment.

You are in charge. If tomorrow you walk into the office and say: 'I want it done this way', the chances are good that it will be. Since you are called names (manager, supervisor, project leader, boss), you have the authority, the power to decide and make changes. If you merely do enough, you are missing a marvellous opportunity to do so much more.

In a large company, your options may be limited by the existing corporate culture – and my advice to you is to act like a crab: face directly into the main thrust of corporate policy and make changes sideways. You do not want to fight the system, but rather to work better within it. In a small company, your options are possibly much wider (since custom is often less rigid) and the impact that you and your team have upon the company's success is proportionately much greater. Thus once you start working well, this will be quickly recognized and nothing gains faster approval than success. But wherever you work, do not be put off by the surprise colleagues will show when you first get serious about managing well.

A SuperManager embraces a personal responsibility for developing his or her own management skills, and for making them work. If you want to get really serious about improving as a manager then you should buy a shiny new notebook to record your ideas and your answers to the questions which this book raises. This is called a *'learning log'* and the simple act of keeping one will help you to focus upon your development. As time goes on, keep looking back to review your old attitudes and practices, and compare them with your new-found common sense.

This book is about personal self-development for enquiring managers. This may mean that you have just been promoted, it may mean that in the last few years you have not actively developed this aspect of your work, or you may simply be an old dog who wants to learn a few new tricks. For whomever you are, this book is going to examine the basic skills of management. By reading and by thinking about these in your own work environment, you will be able to learn rapidly from the simple logic of your experience and practice. So when you come to a little box with the words 'To Practise' in the top left hand corner; do not dither, do it directly.

1.3 Images of a Manager

The whole philosophy of this book is based upon the image of you (a manager) as the leader of a team, a small group of people who work for you in achieving the goals for which you are responsible. What we now must do is to examine what, exactly, is a manager.

> *To Practise 1.1:* yes, here is an exercise (and a quick lesson in solving problems in general). The question is: what do you do as *manager* as distinct from any other part of your job? Write down *ten* items (straight off the top of your head) and then circle the *three* which you feel are the most important in terms of ... no, you choose the criterion.

Throughout this book, you are free to disagree with anything and everything which is written. If in the end you arrive at a completely contrary philosophy, then this book will have succeeded in enabling you to think through and evolve that viewpoint. The book raises questions and offers suggestions; you decide on the answers. Your answers to the exercise are probably completely different from mine, because your company, your character, your peculiar (meaning distinct rather than odd) problems are totally different from mine – or are they? I view a manager as having three roles:

| PLANNER – PROVIDER – PROTECTOR |

The Manager as Planner
The manager has to take a long-term view; indeed, the higher you rise, the further you will have to look. While a team member will be working towards known and established goals, the manager must look further ahead so that these goals are selected wisely. By thinking about the eventual consequences of different plans, the manager selects the optimal plan for the

team and implements it. By taking account of the needs not only of the next project but also the project after that, the manager ensures that work is not repeated nor problems tackled too late, and that the necessary resources are arranged and allocated.

The Manager as Provider

The manager has access to information and materials which the team needs. Often he/she has the authority or influence to acquire things which no one else in the team could. This role for the manager is important simply because no one else can do the job; there is some authority which the manager holds uniquely within the team, and the manager must exercise this to help the team to work.

The Manager as Protector

The team needs security from the vagaries of less enlightened managers. In any company, there are short-term excitements which can deflect the workforce from the important issues. The manager should be there to guard against these distractions and to protect the team. If a new project emerges which is to be given to your team, you are responsible for costing it (especially in terms of time) so that your team is not given an impossible deadline. If someone in your team brings forward a good plan, you must ensure that it receives a fair hearing and that your team knows and understands the outcome. If someone in your team has a problem at work, you have to deal with it.

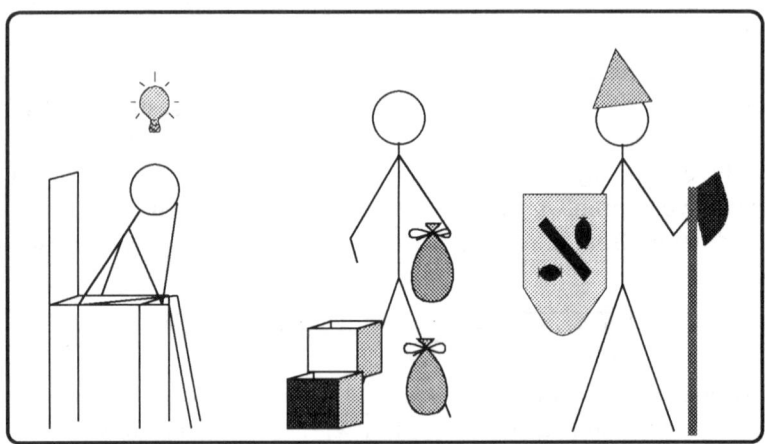

Version Two
That was rather formal. If you like formal, then you are happy. If you do not like formal then here is an alternative answer. A manager is there to provide:

> VISION – VALUES – VERVE

Vision in that the future must be seen and communicated to the team; Values in that the team needs a unifying code of practice which supports and enhances co-operation; Verve in that positive enthusiasm is the best way of making the work exciting and fun. If you do not think your work is exciting, then we have already found a problem – to which we will return in later chapters. A better word than Verve might be *Chutzpah* (except that it does not begin with a 'V') which means 'shameless audacity'. Is that not refreshing? Inspiring even? A manager should dare to do what he/she has decided, and to do it with confidence and pride.

> *To Practise 1.2:* Consider your team and think of the least dynamic individual within it. Let us call him Arnold. What does Arnold know about your Vision for the team? Does Arnold have a clear understanding of the Values which you would wish your team to embrace? When was the last time Arnold said to anyone: 'I'm really enjoying the work at the moment'?

Wait! Before you put the book down, ask yourself this: if Arnold really did enjoy his work, or if he actually felt part of the team's future, would he not work so much better? Now answer the questions honestly and consider how, *tomorrow*, you might do something for Arnold.

1.4 A General Approach

Throughout this book there will be a distant tune playing in the background. Once you hear this tune, you will start humming it to yourself: in the shower, in the boardroom, on the way to work, when watching the sunrise. It is a simple tune which repeats again and again in every aspect of your managerial life; it goes:

> PLAN – MONITOR – REVIEW

Everything you do follows this pattern. It is like a wheel rolling along with all of your projects and tasks. And, of course, it is just common sense. In the centre of this revolving wheel is the Aim. With all decision making, you have to focus very carefully upon the desired outcome; establishing the actual aim can be half the battle.

Before you start any activity you must STOP and THINK about it: what is the objective, how can it be achieved, what are the alternatives, who needs to be involved, what will it cost, is it worth doing? When you have a plan, you should STOP and THINK about how to ensure that your plan is working. You must devise ways to monitor your progress, even if only by setting deadlines for intermediate stages, or counting customer replies, or tracking the number of soggy biscuits which have to be thrown away – whatever, choose something which displays progress and establish a procedure to ensure that happens. But before you start, set a date on which you will STOP and reTHINK your plan in the light of your monitoring.

The last point is so vital, and so often missed. Typically, a bad plan is followed until the consequences become intolerable; by setting a review date and collecting data, you can catch the errors sooner, before any real (or noticed) damage is done.

It is worth stressing the relative importance of the *review*. In an ideal world where managers are wise, information is unambiguous and always available, and changes in life are never abrupt or large; it would be possible for you to sit down and to *plan* the strategy for your group. Unfortunately, managers are mortals, information is seldom complete and always inaccurate (or too voluminous to assimilate), and the unexpected always arrives inconveniently. The situation is never seen in black and white but merely in a fog of various shades of grey. Your planning thus represents no more than the best guess you can make in the current situation; the review is when you interpret the results to deduce the emerging, successful strategy (which might not be the one you had expected). The review is not merely to fine-tune your plan, it is to evaluate the experiment and to incorporate the new, practical information which you have gathered into the creation of the next step forward. You must be prepared for a radical change of direction – indeed this might best be your aim.

Management is often like being lost in a dense forest where all you can do is follow faint paths and climb trees. If you blunder off along the faint paths, you will probably find the other managers who have gone before you; or their bones. If at each review, however, you climb the tallest tree and tie a bright yellow ribbon to the top – you will be able to judge your progress and change your direction (strategy) accordingly. And, common sense dictates, the harder the going, the more frequent are your reviews. Your view may not extend to the end of the project, but at least you are not stumbling around in circles.

> *To Practise 1.3:* Common sense, but not so common. Consider the last full day you spent at work. Write a list of all projects and tasks on which you worked. Next to each, write how it is being monitored and how/when it will next be reviewed. Often it is not what we do, but the way we do it. For each item on the list decide what is the immediate aim (e.g. to analysis some data; to talk to Arthur) and write down an alternative way of doing it (e.g. use graphs instead of just figures; fax a message instead). How often have you done this before?

1.5 Management Skills

This book is descriptive, not prescriptive; you choose your own answers. We are going to rehearse the basic ideas about basic management skills. What follows is a potted tour of management skills with overviews, hints and suggestions. Each chapter can be read separately so you can play around with the order as the mood takes you – but you should read them all.

A manager should focus upon three basic skills:

- Organization   (Time Management, Quality, Project Planning)
- Communication   (Presentation, Writing, Conversation)
- Leadership   (Team Work, Delegation, People)

... and that is what this book is about, with a few extras to help you personally. None of these topics can be viewed in isolation, but we will focus upon each in turn in the next nine chapters.

Organization is about providing a plan and a structure to help you and your team to get the job done. By providing a structure to the activity, you can support and encourage your team since they will know where they are, and what they should do. It allows you to pace, and so to stretch, the amount of work – and to select the work to bring the greatest overall efficiency. Thus organization is concerned with the work, your own time, and the team's time; and as a manager you must be prepared to spend time to save time for your team. Even if you spend all your time organizing others, you may together achieve far more than without that organization. This is not simply a question of allocating tasks. The important point is that the tasks should be structured and allocated so that they match the ability, experience and development needs of each person to whom they are given. Thus the work itself becomes the route to staff motivation and training.

Communication is the most important skill of management since the implementation of all others depends upon it. A manager has to be able to communicate through writing, formal presentations, interviews, specifications and simply in day-to-day conversation – and that communication has to be error free, or time and effort will be wasted. Not only must you be clear in what you say, but you must ensure that what you mean to say is understood; and that what you understand is what was meant.

Leadership is a very nebulous concept. In the last analysis it is about getting people to work for you with total commitment; it is getting them to follow you. The approach which this book advocates is leadership through building your group into a team so that all their talents are working together and with you.

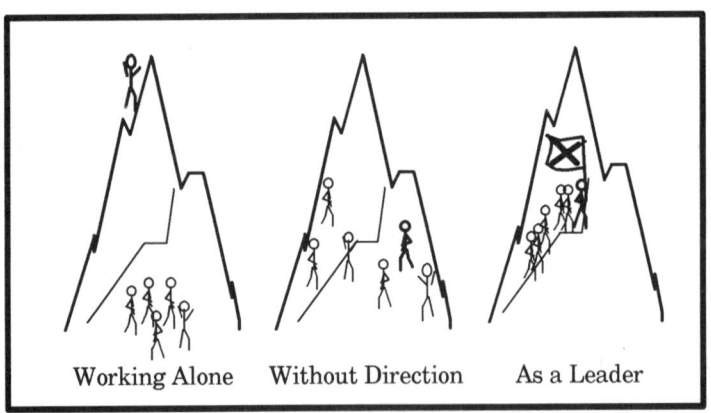

Working Alone   Without Direction   As a Leader

The theory goes as follows:
1) Whipped galley slaves are not nearly as effective as dedicated warriors pulling for the Motherland.
2) Your team has qualities and abilities which they want, and indeed expect, to use – you must ensure that these talents are cultivated or you will lose.

3) What you know is limited; what your team knows is far greater; only by involving the team in the decision making will you use that greater knowledge.

Without a team approach, your staff never gain a common purpose and may never get started. Without being given direction, they may merely wander. You, as manager, must lead them whither they should go.

1.6 To Begin

Becoming a great manager is *easy* because it is only common sense. Once the issues are thought through, your common sense will support your management needs.

Becoming a great manager is *hard* because it is only common sense. You have actually to apply the ideas in practice rather than merely acknowledge that they are good. Initially this means deliberate effort; in the long term it means reminding yourself again and again to stop and think. Of course, if you manage this process itself, you will be able to devise a plan to ensure that you own management development is monitored and reviewed (preferably using your notebook).

The best place to apply these ideas, and to develop your own, is at work. So the first thing to do is to play a game of '*Watch the Manager*':

Step 1: at work, consider the people around you with management responsibility and consider their strengths (not their weaknesses – only their strengths).

Step 2: using the four triplet images of a manager in the summary at the end of this chapter, consider whether each person displays the various qualities shown.

Step 3: for each person draw a pie chart (a circle) with three segments displaying the relative proportions of each quality for each manager (i.e. four pies each).

Step 4: relate (if you can) these charts to your answers to Practice Box 1.1.

Step 5: finally consider Arnold (remember Arnold?) and try to imagine what he would be saying about you if he were doing this exercise himself. If you are brave, why not ask him?

Summary of Beginning

You have the power to define your own
working practices and environment

IMAGES OF A MANAGER

Planner - Provider - Protector

Vision - Values - Verve (Chutzpah)

Organization - Communication - Leadership

add your own
<- three here

PLAN - MONITOR - REVIEW

COMMUNICATION	LEADERSHIP	ORGANIZATION
Presentations	Team Work	Time Management
(chap 2)	*(chap 3)*	*(chap 4)*
Writing	Delegation	Quality
(chap 5)	*(chap 6)*	*(chap 7)*
Conversation	People	Project Planning
(chap 8)	*(chap 9)*	*(chap 10)*

Remember Arnold   **'Watch the Manager'**

Chapter: 2
Formal Presentations

You get the impression that their normal condition is silence and that speech is a slight fever which attacks them now and then
(Jean-Paul Satre)

Presentations are one of the first ordeals which a new manager has to suffer. They are one of the most commonly used methods of communication since they allow large numbers of people to listen at one time to information coming from a few, and the mere formality of the event enhances the attention which people pay to the performance: they all sit still and listen for a change.

Each presentation allows a manager to make a lasting impression upon the audience. It is imperative that this is not a bad impression – and it is a wasted opportunity if it is unremarkable. If management is the art of getting things done, then presentations are a fast and potentially effective method of getting things done through other people. They can be used for expressing or evaluating ideas, conducting discussions, inspiring the team and obtaining the approval of senior management. In terms of your management of a small team you can use presentations to build your team and to plan, monitor and review their progress.

This chapter looks at the presentations in a formal setting. It is a long chapter since giving good presentations is a vital skill which you can develop at your own pace (without necessarily involving your team). Of course, as you improve you will be able to give encouragement to your team members as they too learn, from your example. Further, the communication techniques in giving a good, formal presentation can also be applied to every other form of verbal interaction – so you learn the techniques for the formal setting in the expectation that you will use them all the time.

2.1 Why Bother?

Let us look at this another way: what can a presentation do for you?

Firstly, a presentation puts you on display. Your staff need to see evidence of decisive planning and leadership so that they have confidence in you as their manager. They need to be motivated and inspired to undertake the tasks which you are presenting. Other managers need to understand the merits of your project, and the nature of any help they should offer. Senior management should be impressed by your skill and ability so that they provide the resources, so that you and your team can get the job done.

Secondly, a presentation allows you to ask questions and to initiate discussion. It may not be suitable within the presentation formats of your company to hold a discussion during the presentation itself; but it does allow you to raise the issues, present the problems and at least to establish who amongst the audience could provide valuable input to your decision making.

Finally, a presentation can be fun. They are your chance to speak your mind, to strut your stuff and to tell the people what the world is really like. While you hold the stage, the audience is bound by good manners to sit quietly and watch the performance.

> *To Practise 2.1:* You need a topic. If you have to give a presentation soon, then use that topic; if not, take something from a personal hobby which might interest your friends. Write down the topic (in your notebook) so that it is fixed – phrase it in terms of the title by which you might announce it to staff and friends.

Now comes the frightening bit. Before you start thinking about improving your skills in presentation, it is wise to see how good (or otherwise) you are already. This will allow you to test the extent of the problem and to monitor (through comparison) your progress (which will be dramatic). If you can borrow/buy/hire a video recorder do so, otherwise borrow a good friend who will sit in and watch you.

> *To Practise 2.2:* Without too much study of the following text, take your topic and explain it to an audience in *three* minutes – aim to express the main message, clearly and concisely.

If you can video tape the performance mark yourself afterwards using the critique sheet on the next page – if not, trust your friend to do it for you. Note: the worse you appear at first, the greater (and more satisfying) will be your improvement.

PRESENTATION SKILLS – Critique Form

Speaker: *Evaluator:*   *Date:*

The objective is to provide constructive feedback and/or self-evaluation. For each category, circle a number and add a helpful suggestion where appropriate.

Scale: 1=Magic, 2=Very Good, 3=Good, 4=OK, 5=Poor, 6=Worse than poor.

Beginning
Did the opening gain attention?	1 2 3 4 5 6 →
Did it establish the subject of the talk?	1 2 3 4 5 6 →
Did it establish a rapport?	1 2 3 4 5 6 →

Content
Was the structure clear?	1 2 3 4 5 6 →
Was the main point(s) easily identifiable?	1 2 3 4 5 6 →
Were there helpful examples/analogies?	1 2 3 4 5 6 →
Was there the right amount of material?	1 2 3 4 5 6 →

Ending
Was the main point(s) clearly emphasized?	1 2 3 4 5 6 →
Was the conclusion clear?	1 2 3 4 5 6 →
Was there an effective end?	1 2 3 4 5 6 →

Presentation
Was it audible?	1 2 3 4 5 6 →
Was contact maintained with the audience?	1 2 3 4 5 6 →
Was the delivery fluent?	1 2 3 4 5 6 →
Was there tonal variation?	1 2 3 4 5 6 →
Was it interesting?	1 2 3 4 5 6 →
Did the speaker make an impression?	1 2 3 4 5 6 →

Visual Aids
Were they clear?	1 2 3 4 5 6 →
Were they useful?	1 2 3 4 5 6 →
Were there the right number?	1 2 3 4 5 6 →

Finally
What was the BEST aspect of the presentation?

What aspect would most benefit from improvement – and how?

2.2 The Plan

It is difficult to over-estimate the importance of careful preparation. Five minutes on the floor in front of senior management could decide the acceptance of a proposal of several months' duration for you and your whole team. With so much potentially at stake, the presenter must concentrate not only upon the facts being presented but upon the style, pace, tone and, ultimately, the tactics. As a rule of thumb: for an average presentation, no less than one hour should be spent in preparation for each five minutes of talking.

Suppose you have a talk to give, where do you start?

Objective of a Presentation

The single most important observation is that the objective of a presentation is not the transmission of the message but rather its reception. The whole preparation, presentation and content of a speech must therefore be geared not to the speaker but to the audience. The presentation of a perfect project plan is a failure if the audience do not understand or are not persuaded of its merits. A customers' tour is a waste of time if they leave without realizing the full worth of your product. The objective of communication is to make your message understood and *remembered*.

The main problem with this objective is, of course, the audience: the people who must understand and remember. The average human being has a very short attention span and a million other things to think about. Your job in the presentation is to reach through this mental fog and to hold the attention long enough to make your point.

Formulate your Aims

The starting point in planning any speech is to formulate a precise aim. This should take the form of a simple, concise statement of intent. For example, the purpose of your speech may be to obtain funds, to evaluate a proposal, or to motivate your team. No two aims will be served equally well by the same presentation; and if you are not sure at the onset what you are trying to do, it is unlikely that your plan will achieve it.

One question is: how many different aims can you achieve, in say, thirty minutes – and the answer: not many. In the end, it is far more productive to achieve one goal than to blunder through several. The best approach is to isolate the essential aim and to list at most two others which can be addressed providing they do not distract from the main one. *Focus is key.* If you do not focus upon your aim, it is unlikely that the audience will.

> *To Practise 2.3:* For your talk, select an aim. This is not just a restatement of the title, it is the answer to the question: 'what do you want to be the consequence of your talk?'

Identify the Audience
The next task is to consider the audience to determine how best to achieve your aim in the context of these people.

Suppose your talk is on the leadership style of Machiavelli. If you think your audience knows little history, you might include some background on 15-16th century Florence; if the audience has high standards of political correctness, you might shock them with some of his most 'morally questionable' ideas; if they are romantics, talk of Princes and Power; if they are pragmatists, talk of outcomes; if they are politicians, talk of practical applications in the current day. Essentially, you must consider the topic from the point of view of the audience and provide them with the information they lack, emphasizing the aspects in which they will be most interested.

Another way of preparing for an audience is to try to identify their aims in attending your presentation. If you can somehow convince them that they are achieving their aims while you achieve yours, you will find a helpful and receptive audience. For instance, if you are seeking approval for a new product plan from senior management it is useful to know and understand their main objectives. If they are currently worried that their product range is out of date and old fashioned, you would emphasize the innovative aspects of your new product; if they are fearful about product diversification, you would then emphasize how well your new product fits within the existing catalogue.

This principle of matching the audience's aims, however, goes beyond the simple salesmanship of an idea – it is the simplest and most effective manner for obtaining their attention at the beginning. If your opening remarks imply that you understand their problem and that you have a solution, then they will be flattered by your attention and attentive to your every word.

The size of a group can also affect your presentation styles and techniques. If the presentation is to be a cosy boardroom chat around a warm coffee pot and crumpets with only three or four people present, then your style will be informal and possibly targeted at those specific individuals; on the other hand, if you are addressing a formal boardroom meeting of shareholders and executive officers, then your presentational style will need to be crisp, sharp, and efficient with as much starch as in the collar you will undoubtedly be wearing. The mix of people is also important, since your speech will need to have something for everybody. If this proves too difficult, remember your original aim and identify the sub-groups of the audience through whom it will best be achieved. This is particularly relevant to getting project approval in those organizations where the final decision rests with one individual alone; this is where you target the speech.

> *To Practise 2.4.* Using the same topic as before, construct three different approaches to explaining it: 1) to your manager's manager, 2) to a class of twelve-year-olds, 3) to your team at work.

2.3 Structure

All speeches should have a definite structure or format. A talk without a structure is a woolly mess. If you do not structure your thoughts, the audience will not be able to follow them. Having established the aim of your presentation you should choose the most appropriate structure for achieving it.

Sequential Argument
One of the simplest structures is that of sequential argument which consists of a series of linked statements ultimately leading to a conclusion. This can also be one of the most bland. It is commonly used by university lecturers and is characterized by a monotonous exposition where each topic is run one into the next without any clear definition or boundaries between them.

These are the pitfalls. However, sequential argument is a valid structure and when used properly can be very powerful. That power lies in its simplicity and this simplicity can only be achieved by careful and deliberate delineation between each section. One technique is the use of frequent reminders to the audience of the main point which has preceded and an explicit explanation of how the next topic will lead on from this.

Hierarchical Decomposition
This is the classical method of presentation where the main topic is broken down into sub-topics and each sub-topic into smaller topics until eventually everything is broken down into very small basic units. In this manner, the presentation takes the same form as a book which is broken down into chapters, sections, sub-sections, sub-topics, paragraphs, etc. In written communication this is a very powerful technique because it allows the reader to re-order the presentation at will, and to return to omitted topics at a later

date. In verbal communication the audience is restricted to the order of the presenter and so the structure can only be useful if it is clearly understood and reinforced for the audience.

One technique, therefore, is to display and explain the structure at the beginning of the talk and to preface each sub-section by re-displaying the current position within the defined hierarchy. As with sequential argument it is useful to summarize each section at its conclusion and to introduce each major, new section with a statement of how it lies in the hierarchical order.

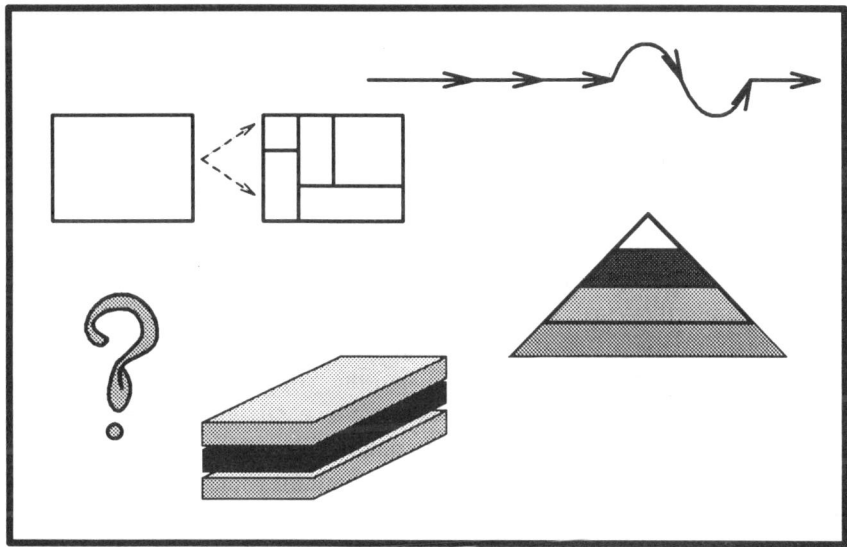

Question Orientated

The aim of many presentations given by managers is either to explain a previous decision or to seek approval for a plan of action. In these cases, the format can be question-orientated. The format is to introduce the problem and any relevant background, and then to outline the various solutions explaining the advantages and disadvantages of each solution in turn. Finally, all possible options are summarized in terms of their pros and cons, and either the preferred solution is presented for endorsement by the audience or a discussion is initiated leading to a decision. One trick for obtaining the desired outcome is to suggest during the presentation the criteria by which the various options are to be judged; this alone should allow you to obtain the outcome you desire.

Pyramid
In a newspaper, the story is introduced in its entirety in a catchy first paragraph. The next few paragraphs repeat the same information only giving further details to each point. The next section repeats the entire story again, but developing certain themes within each of the sub-points and again adding more information. This is repeated until the reporter runs out of embellishments. The editor then simply decides upon the newsworthiness of the report and cuts from the bottom to the appropriate number of column inches.

In terms of presentations, the television news is a better example. At the beginning of each major story there is a complete summary – then there follows a fuller report, usually from an outside reporter complete with location footage. This itself may be similarly broken down into smaller pyramids. Finally, there is that seemingly personal summary or observation to conclude the report.

There are two main advantages to this style for presentations. Firstly, it can increase the audience's receptiveness to the main ideas since at every stage of the pyramid they have already become familiar with the ideas and indeed know what to expect next. This sense of *déjà vu* can falsely give the impression that what they are hearing are their own opinions. The second advantage is that the duration of the talk can be easily altered by cutting the talk in exactly the same way as the newspaper editor might have done to the news story. This degree of flexibility may be useful if the same presentation is to be used several times in different situations.

The Meaty Sandwich
The simplest and most direct format remains the meaty sandwich. This is the simple beginning-middle-end format in which the main meat of the exposition is contained in the middle and is preceded by an introduction and followed by a summary and conclusion. This is really the appropriate format for all small sub-sections in all the previous structures. If the talk is short enough, or the topic simple enough, it can form the structure of the whole presentation.

> *To Practise 2.5:* At the end of this chapter you will want to repeat your original talk – only this time aiming for *twelve* minutes. You know the title, you know your audience, you have an aim. Now choose a structure. You should thus arrive at an outline or skeleton of your entire talk (no details yet), possibly using one or more of the above structures.

Finally, the structure must not get in the way of the main message. If it is too complex, too convoluted or simply too noticeable, the audience will be distracted. If a section is unnecessary to achieving your fundamental aim, pluck it out.

2.4 The Beginning

There are so many people who will tell you that the first few seconds of any encounter are the most important. For instance some people claim to be able to judge an interview candidate before he/she has even sat down (but do not let these people do interviews!). It is imperative to plan your beginning carefully so that you start on a winning course. There are five main elements:

Get their attention
Too often in a speech, the first few minutes of the presentation are lost while people adjust their coats, drift in with coffee and finish the conversation they were having with the person next to them. You only have a limited time and every minute is precious to you. So, from the beginning, make sure they pay attention.

Establish a theme
Basically, you need to start the audience thinking about the subject matter of your presentation. This can be done by a statement of your main objective, unless for some reason you want to keep it hidden. Each member of the audience will have some previous experience of, and an opinion about, your subject; you should make them recall these at the beginning.

One device both to get their attention and to establish the theme is to use the rhetorical question. Something like: 'Who can think of a simple change to allow us to penetrate a totally new market?' Another possibility is to start with an informative or amusing quotation.

Present the structure
If you explain briefly at the beginning of a talk how it is to proceed then the audience will know what to expect. This can help to establish the theme and also provide something concrete to hold their attention. Ultimately, it provides a sense of security in the promise that this speech too will end.

Create a rapport

If you can win the audience over in the first minute, you will keep them for the remainder. You should plan exactly how you wish to appear to them and use the beginning to establish that relationship. You may be presenting yourself as their friend, as an expert, perhaps even as a judge, but whatever role you choose you must establish it at the very beginning.

One approach in creating a rapport is to introduce yourself and to establish for the audience why it is you and not somebody else who is giving this talk. If you have worked on a similar project before remind them; if you studied the topic at a training course tell them about it; if you have been monitoring the progress of the project refer to that fact. This is the difficult balance of persuading the audience that they should be listening to you, without appearing condescending or smug.

Administration

When planning your presentation you should make a note to find out if there are any administrative details which need to be announced at the beginning of your speech. This is not simply to make yourself popular with the people organizing the session but also because, if these details are over-looked, the audience may become distracted as they wonder what is going to happen next.

One question of administration which should be resolved at the beginning is when questions would be welcomed. If you do not wish to be interrupted, then say: 'I will ask for questions at the end'. If you would like to clarify any points as they occur, then say: 'Please feel free to ask questions during the course of the presentation'; you may, of course, withdraw this invitation later.

2.5 The Ending

The final impression you make on the audience is the one they will remember; thus, it is worth planning your last few sentences with extreme care.

As with the beginning, it is necessary first to get their attention, which will have wandered. This requires a change of pace, a new visual aid, or perhaps the introduction of one final, culminating idea. In some formats the ending will be a summary of the main points of the talk. One of the greatest mistakes is to tell the audience that this is going to be a summary because at that moment they simply switch off. Indeed it is sometimes best for the ending to come unexpectedly with that final vital phrase left hanging in the air and ringing round their memories. Alternatively the ending can be a flourish, with the pace and voice leading the audience through the final crescendo to the inescapable conclusion.

There are two techniques which work effectively. The first relies upon the formation of a simple, clear, concise and memorable phrase which contains the message of your presentation. This can be introduced with a phrase such as, 'I will leave you with one final thought: ...' or, 'It simply comes down to this: ...'. The second is to use the rhetorical question, asking the audience what is the solution to their problem (even if they did not know that they had a problem), and then listing the conclusions you reached in the main body of the presentation.

> *To Practise 2.6:* Considering, at all times, the aim of your talk, *write out* the beginning and end of your talk. These should be 50-250 words each.

2.6 Visual Aids

Most people expect visual reinforcement to any verbal message being delivered. While it would be unfair to blame television entirely for this, it is useful to understand to what the audience are accustomed, for two reasons: firstly, you can meet their expectations using the overhead projector, a slide show, or even a video presentation; secondly, if you depart from the framework of a square picture flashed before their eyes, then that novelty will be more arresting. For instance, if you are describing the six functions of a project manager then display the six *hats* he/she must wear; if you are introducing the idea of the team taking part in decision making, then brandish a fishing rod to *fish for* ideas.

With traditional visual aids (such as slides or *viewfoils* for an overhead projector), there are a few rules which should be followed to ensure they are used effectively. Most are common sense, and most are commonly ignored. As with all elements of a speech, each different viewfoil should have a distinct purpose – and if it has no purpose it should be removed. With the purpose firmly in mind you should design the viewfoil for that purpose. Some viewfoils are there to reinforce the verbal message and so to assist in recall; others are used to explain information which can be more easily displayed than described; and some are designed simply for entertainment and thus to pace the presentation.

If your viewfoil is scruffy then your audience will notice that and not what is written upon it. Do not clutter a viewfoil or it will confuse rather than assist. Do not simply photocopy information if there is more data on the page than you need to present; in this case, the data should be extracted before being displayed. Make sure that your foils can be read from the back of the room.

When using visual aids, it is important not to talk to *them*. The presenter who stares down at the visual display unit or, worse, turns away from the audience and stares at the screen is making no contact with the audience and will lose their attention.

> *To Practise 2.7:* Design a visual aid, or something you might draw on a flip-chart, to illustrate the main message of your talk. Concentrate on making the message as clear and *memorable* as possible.

2.7 The Delivery

The human body is truly fascinating – there are some I could watch all day (Anon)

Whatever you say and whatever you show, it is you, yourself which will remain the focus of the audience's attention. If you but strut and fret your hour upon the stage and then are gone, no-one will remember what you said. The presenter has the power both to kill the message, and to enhance it a hundred times beyond its worth. Your job as a manager is to use the potential of the presentation to ensure that the audience is motivated and inspired rather than disconcerted or distracted. There are five key facets of the human body which deserve attention in presentation skills: the eyes, the voice, the expression, the appearance, and the stance.

Eyes

The eyes are said to be the key to the soul and are therefore the first and most effective weapon in convincing the audience of your honesty, openness and confidence in the aim of your presentation. This impression may of course be totally false, but here is how to convey it.

Even in casual conversation, your feelings of friendship and intimacy can be evaluated by the intensity and duration of eye contact. During the presentation you should use this to enhance your rapport with the audience by establishing eye contact with each and every member of the audience as often as possible. For small groups this is clearly possible but it can also be achieved with large audiences since the larger the group, the harder it is for them to tell precisely at whom the presenter is looking. Thus by simply staring at a group of people at the back of a lecture theatre it is possible to convince each of them individually that he or she is the object of your attention. You should try the experiment of standing some distance away from a friend and asking him/her to let you know as soon as you are no longer looking directly into his/her eyes. If you then gently allow your eyes to drift away you should be surprised at how far away your gaze can stray before it is noticed. During presentations, try to hold your gaze fixed in specific directions for five or six seconds at a time. Shortly after each change in position, give a slight smile; this will convince each person in that direction that you have seen and acknowledged them.

Voice
Enunciation, pronunciation, tonal pitch and variation, these will all, you must agree, enhance the message, from you to me.

After the eyes comes the voice – and the two most important aspects of the voice for the public speaker are projection and variation. A monotone speech is both boring and soporific, so it is important to try to vary the pitch and speed of your presentation. At the very least, each new sub-section should be preceded by a pause and a change in tone to emphasize the delineation. If tonal variation does not come to you naturally, try making use of rhetorical questions throughout your speech since most accents rise naturally at the end of a question.

It is important to realize from the onset that few people can take their ordinary conversation voice and put it on stage. If you can, then perhaps you should move to Hollywood. The main difference comes in the degree of feedback which you can expect from the person to whom you are talking. In ordinary conversation you can see from the expression, perhaps a subtle movement of the eye, when a word or phrase has been missed or misunderstood. In front of an audience you have to make sure that this never happens. The simple advice is to slow down and to take your time. Remember, the audience is constrained by good manners not to interrupt you, so there is no need to maintain a constant flow of sound. A safe style is to be slightly louder and slightly slower than a fire-side chat with slightly deaf aunt. As you get used to the sound, you can adjust it by watching the audience.

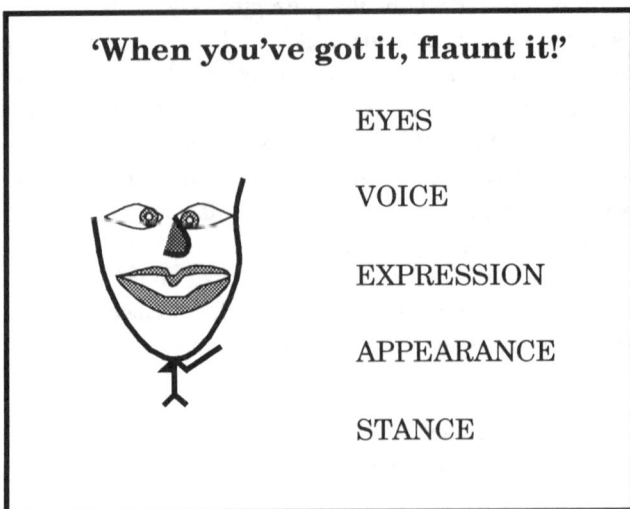

Expression

The audience watch your face. If you are looking listless or distracted then they will be listless and distracted. If you are smiling, they will wonder why. If you pronounce your speech without hearing it yourself, then your face will remain blank throughout and a blank face to the audience will be a distraction. Instead you should be aware that in normal conversation your meaning is enhanced by facial reinforcement. Thus, in a speech you must compensate both for stage nerves and for the distance between yourself and the audience by accentuating your facial expressions.

The basic principle is to make friends with each member of the audience. To do this, you will need to achieve a natural presentation and to display a commitment to its message. Both of these are precluded by a lack of facial movement. It is not necessary, nor indeed comfortable, to have a fixed smile throughout the presentation as this would quickly have you marked as a second-hand car salesman. The message is quite simple: make sure that your facial expressions are natural, only more so.

Appearance

There are many guides to management and presentation styles which lay heavy emphasis upon the way you dress and in the last analysis this is a matter of personal choice. That choice should, however, be made deliberately. When you are giving a presentation you must dress for the audience, not for yourself; if they think you look out of place, then you are.

The basic advice is either to dress in such a way that it is not an issue, or to dress to establish a definite point. If you decide to 'power dress' then you must ensure that the presentation style matches, or you will appear a fraud. You should always 'dress smart' for a presentation since this is a mark of courtesy and respect for the audience – you may not think that this matters but if the audience does, and you have not dressed appropriately, then you have lost them. If you do consider rebelling against an established practice, remember that it will convey a subliminal message that you are different (or want to be); this may hinder communication.

Stance and Movement

When an actor initially learns a new character part, he/she will instinctively adopt a distinct posture or stance to convey that character. It follows, therefore, that while you are on stage, your stance and posture will convey a great deal about you. The least you must do is make sure your stance does not convey boredom; at best, you can use your whole body as a dynamic tool to reinforce your rapport with the audience. Whole-body movement can be used by the presenter to maintain the audience's attention and to add emphasis to the main points and sections of a talk. Even walking between the lectern and the projector screen will cause the audience to follow you.

The perennial problem is what to do with your hands. These must not wave aimlessly through the air, or fiddle constantly with a pen. Men should, at all costs, avoid juggling keys or change in their trouser pockets; women should avoid fiddling with jewelry. The trick is to keep your hands still, except when used in unison with your speech. To train them initially, find a safe resting place which is comfortable for you and aim to return them there when any gesture is completed.

2.8 The Techniques of Speech

Every speaker has a set of 'tricks of the trade' which he or she holds dear – the following is a selection of advice taken from various sources.

Make an impression

Three weeks later, your speech will have been forgotten. The most you can hope for is that one phrase, one idea, perhaps even one gesture, will have made an impression upon the audience and will be remembered. The trick is to choose this nebulous something so that it is associated with the main message of your speech.

The average audience is very busy: they have husbands and wives, schedules and slippages, cars and mortgages; and although they will be trying very hard to concentrate on your speech, their minds will inevitably stray. Your job is to do something, anything, which captures their attention and makes a lasting impression upon them. Once you have planned your speech and honed it down to its few salient points, isolate the most important message and devise some method to make it stick.

> *To Practise 2.8:* This is also called finding a hook. Take your aim and devise some hook on which to hang it in the mind of your audience.

Repeat, Repeat
He said it thrice, it must be true
(Lewis Carrol)

The average audience is very busy: they have husbands or wives etc, etc – but repetition makes them hear. The average audience is easily distracted, and their attention will slip during the most important message of your speech – so repeat it. You don't necessarily have to use the resonant tonal sounds of the repeated phrase, but simply make the point again and again and again with different explanations and in different ways. The classic advice of the Sergeant Major is: 'First you tell 'em what you are going to tell 'em, then you tell 'em, then you tell 'em what you told 'em!'

Pace
Try the following experiment next time you are out drinking with friends: talk to them in a very flat, monotone voice without pauses between sentences and without any variation in the speed of your delivery, and watch how long it takes for their attention to drift away. The same boredom is created during a speech, only more so. Yet variation in pace is one of the simplest techniques for delineating various sections and maintaining audiences' interest. If you become animated and excited by the topic then the audience will be curious to find out why. If you pause to collect your thoughts before a new section then the audience too will pause and collect theirs. Essentially, if you can feel that the audience are tiring then give them a break, and then rouse them to the next part of your speech. One cannot say directly to an audience: 'Look at me I am about to say something important', but a change in pace can say it for you.

Draw Signposts

Research into teaching has yielded the following observation: 'We found that students who failed to get the point did so because they were not looking for it' (common sense?). If the audience knows when to listen, they will make a special effort to do so. Thus if you are coming to the main three points of your talk you should tell them. Something like: 'There are three main points: first ..., second ..., and third ...', will tell them what to expect. A useful technique is to run through each point briefly, and then repeat each in turn, in detail; and finally remind them what the three points were.

Draw a Picture

The human brain is used to dealing with images, and this ability can be used to make the message more memorable. This means using metaphors or analogies to express your message. Thus a phrase like 'we need to increase the market penetration before there will be sufficient profits for a pay-related bonus' becomes 'we need a bigger slice of the cake before the feast'. In the last analysis a novel image or picture can be a memorable hook to hold your point.

> *To Practise 2.9:* Think of an image you could use verbally to illustrate your main message.

Humour

The set-piece joke can work very well, but it can also lead to disaster. You must choose a joke which is apt and one which will not offend any member of the audience. This tends to rule out all racist, sexist or generally rude jokes. If this seems to rule out all the jokes you can think of, then you should avoid jokes in a speech.

Amusing asides are also useful in maintaining the attention of the audience, and for relieving the tension of the speech. If this comes naturally to you, then it is a useful tool for pacing your delivery by providing periods of relaxation between your sign-posted major points.

Short and Sweet

One way to polish the presentation of the main point of your speech is to consider it thus. The day before your presentation, you are called to the office of the divisional Vice-President; there you are introduced to the Managing Director and a representative of the company's major shareholder. 'O.K.' says the Vice-President, 'we believe you have got something to say, we'll give you thirty seconds, *GO*'. Can you do it?

30 Starting to Manage

> *To Practise 2.10:* GO, do it NOW; and afterwards spend about ten minutes devising the perfect thirty second speech.

If you can crystallize your thoughts and combine your main message with some memorable phrase or imagery, and present them both in thirty seconds, then you have either the perfect ending or the basis for a fine presentation.

Plain Speech

Yes! The general rule is to use simple words, and to keep sentences brief. No audience will be impressed by a speaker who runs out of breath.

The Stunt

My favourite stunt in a formal presentation comes from a talk on Stress Management. The more formal the setting, the better. To illustrate the potential dangers of untreated stress on the manager's mind, one takes an empty can of fizzy pop and puts it on the table in front of the audience. While everyone looks on, mount the table and stand with one foot on top of the can. It will bear your weight as long as you apply it directly from above. As you stand there, on one leg on an empty can of fizzy pop, you start to tell them about the dangers of stress in management.

The danger of stress is that it builds up gradually; you sort of know it is there but you can still manage. In fact (stepping onto the can) you can put up with a surprisingly large amount of stress without any problems and carry on regardless. The *danger* is that you become more fragile, more susceptible to the unexpected, so that if something unusual happens which normally would not have bothered you at all, if perhaps there is figuratively a slight blow from the side, then ...

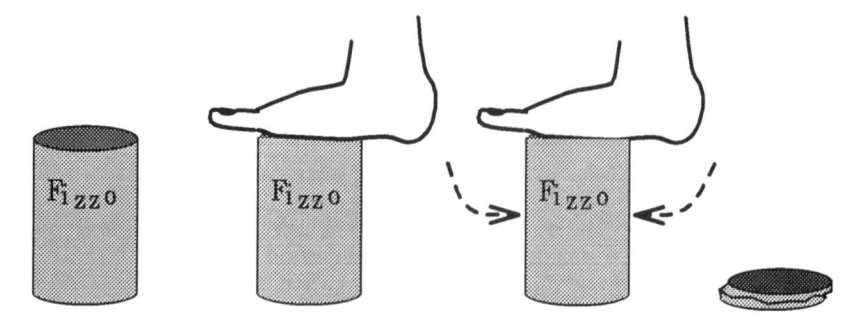

At this stage you bend over (on one leg still) and very gently tap the can from both sides – and the can collapses instantly. Then you pick up the crumpled metal and flourish it aloft saying: '... and this is what happens to the psyche of the over-stressed manager.'

The Narrative

There was once a speaker who was mistakenly asked to address a large dinner at the New Jersey Hilton for a convention of Cattle Ranchers; 'mistakenly' because the theme of his talk was to condemn the use of chemicals in stimulating meat production. He mounted the podium and surveyed the ballroom full of contented diners who had just finished a sumptuous course of *boeuf bourguignon* washed down with a 1979 *Nuits-St-Georges*, and he saw a panorama of well-fed contentment. He waited in silence until everyone was hushed by his slightly sinister stare and then he took from his jacket pocket a small, delicate bottle with a Skull and Cross-Bones on the label, and put it next to the glass of water which had been set beside the lectern for his use. 'I hope,' he started slowly, 'I hope you enjoyed the beef', and he paused as picked up the tiny bottle and drained the last few drops of liquid into his glass; 'I hope,' he continued, 'I hope you did not realize that it contains *poison*,' and he slowly drank the entire contents of his glass, 'because I think it should be your last'.

He did not convert anyone that day; but three people fainted, five left the room in a hurry, and no one in the audience will ever be able to forget that convention. There can be do denying the value of a well constructed stunt in catching the attention of the audience.

Everyone loves a story. Stories can both instruct and convey a message. Zen philosophy is recorded in its stories and Christianity was originally taught in parables. If you can weave your message into a story or a personal anecdote, then you can have them wanting to hear your every word – even if you have to make it up.

> *To Practise 2.11:* Consider your talk and devise an anecdote to make your message memorable.

2.9 The Actual Mechanics

Even with all this planning, we have not yet got to the podium. There are a few more things to deal with to ensure that your communication is unhindered.

Rehearsal

There is no substitute for rehearsal. You can do it in front of a mirror, or to an empty theatre. In both cases, you should accentuate your gestures and vocal projection so that you get used to the sight and sound of yourself. Do not be put off by the mirror – remember: you see a lot less of yourself than your friends do. For a first-time talk, you should run through your speech at least three times, making improvements as you go; if you do not have the time, then make it.

Notes
It is wrong to read out the whole speech unless either: 1) this is the only way you can manage, or 2) you can do so without seeming to. For the novice presenter, it leads to a very pedantic and uninspiring performance.

Try to support your talk with notes – preferably on small cards which can be held unobtrusively. The notes should refer to the decided structure, with the main points clearly written out. These notes are your safety net. Alternatively, if you are using viewfoils, these can often be sufficient notes in themselves.

Any numerical data or quotations should be included in notes as well as on visual aids. The notes will allow you to refer to the data without turning your back on the audience to look at the screen.

Relaxation
It may sound like transcendental meditation but, honestly, if you get nervous just before the show – concentrate on controlling your breathing. An alternative point of view is that nerves are the best possible thing that can happen to you since they get the adrenaline flowing.

The good news is that the audience will not notice your nerves nearly as much as you think. On the same lines, if you lose concentration in the middle of the speech and you do not know what to say next – *smile*, look at your notes, and take your time. The silence will seem long to you, but not to the audience.

Um, Er
Avoid the ums and ers of life. If you are in any doubt as to whether these occur during your speech, plant a friend in the audience and get them to count how many times you say 'er' or 'um' or any other verbal punctuation such as 'sort of' or 'like' or 'you know' or 'right' or 'OK' or ... Remember, silence is golden and can be a welcome break for the audience.

Dealing with Questions
This can be one of the most challenging aspects of your talk; there is always someone else who wants their say. The first thing to realize is that preparing for questions is part of preparing for your talk; you should try to guess what you might be asked and prepare your answers in advance.

If you are asked a question in front of a large group, it is polite to repeat the question to ensure that everyone has heard it – this also give you longer to think of an answer. Keep your answers short (unless you want to block other questions) because now the agenda is moving away from the one you had prepared; the question may not interest the majority of the audience, and you may be caught out on unfamiliar (unprepared) ground. If the answer deserves to be long, précis it and offer to meet the questioner afterwards over coffee.

If you do not know the answer, say so honestly because there is a very good chance that the (interested) questioner does know the answer, and wants to catch you out. Once you have admitted your ignorance you should offer to find out the information and ask the questioner to leave a phone number.

If you know of areas which you wish to avoid, do not ignore them but decide beforehand how to dodge. Particularly useful is to repeat the question and then to answer another (politicians do this all the time). Stroking the questioner is also useful, by saying something like: 'that is a particularly interesting question', or 'I'm glad you raised that'. This allows them to have some of the recognition they were probably seeking and so makes them less likely to press on with an attack.

Time Keeping
It is initially very difficult to prejudge the length of your material. There are two conflicting tendencies: 1) to race through the material, 2) to be easily side-tracked, especially by audience interruptions. It is therefore essential to keep track of time. This can be done using two devices: either take off your watch and lay it by your notes, or ask someone in the audience to let you know when you are a few minutes before the end of the allotted time. Preferably both of these should be used as a safety precaution.

Check the Beginning and the End
As any conductor of an amateur orchestra will tell you, if you begin well and end well, the middle will be forgiven. This being understood, you should put a lot of effort into the opening and the ending. Try out a few different ones.

The opening is important to you not only because it establishes your subject and your rapport with the audience, but also because it is the first thing you say. This may make or break your nerve for the whole talk, so rehearse the opening a few extra times.

The ending is where you can remind the audience of what you had meant them to hear in the middle. This is the last impression you make upon them, so if you can think of something succinct and memorable for your last few phrases – learn them well, and rehearse.

Beforehand
Always, always, always check the hall and equipment in advance. Try out the acoustics, learn how to use the microphone (if there is one), make sure the overhead-projector has a bulb in it, decide where to stand so that you can best be seen and heard. Nineteen times out of twenty there will be no problems, but when you forestall even one calamity this way, you too will preach this practice for life.

Plan   Mon - i - tor   Re - view

Afterwards
Once the speech is over and you have calmed down, you should try to honestly evaluate your performance. Either alone, or with the help of a friend in the audience, decide what was the least successful aspect of your presentation and resolve to concentrate on that point in the next talk you give. KEEP A LOG OF THESE POINTS in your notebook. If it is a problem associated with the preparation, then deal with it there; if it is a problem with your delivery, write yourself a reminder note and put it in front of you at the next talk. Practice is only productive when you make a positive effort to improve.

> *To Practise 2.12:* Now you have to plan and perform the *twelve-minute* version of your speech. Go back over each of the suggestions in the last two sections and decide which of them benefit you and your communication; choose which to use. Try to give your talk to the same friend or video camera as before, and celebrate each and every improvement.

2.10 Constant Learning

Developing your presentation skills brings a whole new excitement to bored meetings, and a new dimension to our game of *'Watch the Manager'*. From now on, when you are watching any presentation, you should start looking for ideas. As a suggestion, try to establish in each talk the single most important message, and then how it was actually presented.

The critique form given earlier is a good way of finding the best techniques (which you might copy) and those most in need of improvement (which you might treat as an exercise). It might be impolitic to actually bring this into meetings, however, but at least look for the best and the worst aspect of each talk.

In terms of feedback to your own team, you might start making comments upon presentations. Not as a sudden judgement from on high in front of the assembled court, but as a personal comment afterwards which others may/should overhear so as to make the feedback less intimidating and to spread the word. Always say what you liked best: 'you made that point very clearly', 'that viewfoil worked particularly well'; and then follow with a concrete suggestion on how to improve the main deficiency (if there is one).

For yourself, start giving talks. Not only the ones you have to give, but also others. You must force yourself onto the platform to gain experience and confidence, and you MUST force yourself to allocate time and effort to the preparation. Once you have conquered formal presentations, you will find that your views are more often heard and your opinion more often sought – simply because you are known as an effective communicator.

Summary of Presentations

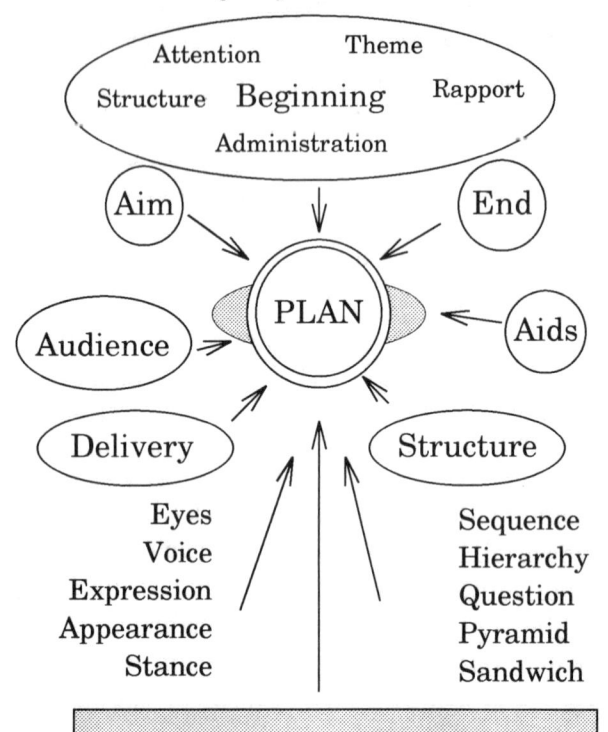

Beginning
- Attention
- Theme
- Structure
- Rapport
- Administration

PLAN
- Aim
- End
- Audience
- Aids
- Delivery
- Structure

Delivery
- Eyes
- Voice
- Expression
- Appearance
- Stance

Structure
- Sequence
- Hierarchy
- Question
- Pyramid
- Sandwich

- Impression
- Repetitition
- Pace
- Sign posts
- Picture
- Humour
- Plain speaking
- Short and Sweet
- Narrative
- Stunt
- Rehearsal
- Notes
- RELAX
- Timing
- Er Um
- Questions

Chapter: 3
Team Work

Teams used to consist of mules – it is time for a new approach
(Anon)

In the beginning, God made an individual – and then He made a pair. The pair formed a group, together they begat others and thus the group grew. But the group did not work well together due to differences of opinions, arguments, preferential treatment; and the group disintegrated in conflict. Cain then settled in the land of Nod – and there has been trouble in groups ever since.

In most companies, the organization is structured in layers of small groups where each group reports to a manager who is also in a group reporting to a manager who is also ... and so on. Thus the whole success of the company can depend upon the manner in which these groups are managed. It would be nice if the whole company suddenly understood that by explicit team building it could increase the potential of its workforce dramatically – but until this happens, you (as the enlightened manager) will have to concentrate upon your own team and its development. Fortunately, this means that they (and so you) will shine in comparison with all other groups in the company – once you have built them into a team.

The basic idea is that you want your team not simply to work on the tasks you give them as *individuals* but rather in a *collective* effort where the best talents of all are matched against each task. In this way they interact to support, help, pool experience and ideas, and in general drive themselves forward. There are ways of looking at teams, of building them up so that they grow together, of tapping that power of mutual support and encouragement. Yet the surprised manager knows little of these things, and without a little learning that potential will be lost.

In this chapter, we examine two perspectives on the theory of co-operative group work to gain an understanding of the underlying process, and look at how you can accelerate the development of your own team.

3.1 Why a Group?

When people work in groups, there are two quite separate issues involved. Firstly there is the *task*, often ill-defined and misunderstood, but always the something which the group is trying to get done. Unfortunately, this is often the only issue which the group considers. On the other hand, there is also the group *process*: the mechanisms, practices, techniques by which the group works and acts together – and if these working practices are ignored, they are unlikely to be optimal. Without due attention to the group process, the value of the group can be diminished or even destroyed; yet with a little explicit management of the process, it can enhance the worth of the group to be many times the sum of the worth of its individuals. It is this *synergy* which makes group work attractive, despite the possible problems (and time spent) in group formation.

A group of people working in the same room, or even on a common project, does not necessarily invoke the group process. If the group is managed in a totally autocratic manner, there may be little opportunity for interaction relating to the work; if there are feuding factions within the group, the process may never evolve. In simple terms, the group process leads to a spirit of cooperation, coordination and commonly understood procedures and mores. If this is present within a group of people, then their performance will be enhanced by their mutual support (both practical and moral). If you think this is a nebulous concept when applied to the world of industry, consider the effect that a self-opinionated, cantankerous loud-mouth would have on your own team's performance and then contrast that to working with a group of friendly, open, helpful colleagues.

A group can be seen as a self-managing unit. Because of the range of skills and the self monitoring, a group can safely be given delegated responsibility. Even if a problem could be solved by a single person, there are two main benefits in involving the people who will carry out the decision. Firstly, the motivational aspect of participating in the decision will clearly enhance its implementation. Secondly, there may well be factors which the implementers understand better than the single person who could supposedly have decided alone.

More indirectly, if your team members become trained, through participation in group decision making, in an understanding of your objectives and work practices, then they will each be better able to make decisions about their own work. And since they have practised the use of authority in a group, they may be given it individually as is exemplified in the celebrated right of Japanese car workers to halt the production line.

Groups are particularly good at combining talents and providing innovative solutions to possibly unfamiliar problems. In cases where there is no well established approach/procedure, the wider skill and knowledge set of the group has a distinct advantage over that of the individual. In general, however, there is an overriding advantage in a group-based work force which makes it attractive: groups work harder.

From the individual's point of view, there is the added incentive that through belonging to a group each can participate in achievements well beyond his/her own individual potential. Less idealistically, the group provides an environment where the individual's self-perceived level of responsibility and authority is enhanced, while accountability is shared, thus providing a perfect motivator through enhanced self-esteem coupled with low stress.

As a manager, you must view the group process as an important resource in itself whose maintenance must be managed just like any other resource. The trick is to enable the team to undertake this management so that it forms a normal part of the team's own activity. Thus, they too must understand the basics of group work, so that with any group activity the first questions are not about the task but rather about how to organize the group.

> *To Practise 3.1:* Take a good look at your group. How often do you hear suggestions from them? How willing is each person to help out with another's task? If someone had expertise in one field, would they volunteer it to help another? If you had a problem about which you knew little, would you turn to the group for suggestions? If not, why not?

3.2 Group Roles

One way of thinking about groups is to examine the various roles undertaken within them. These are simply pigeon-holes for the various functions performed in any group – each person fulfils several roles to varying degrees.

1) *Company worker*: keeps the interests of the organization to the fore at all times.
2) *Chair*: ensures that the views of all participants are heard, and keeps things moving.
3) *Shaper*: follows particular lines of argument and blends together elements of the contributions from several other members.
4) *Ideas person*: contributes novel suggestions.
5) *Resource investigator*: assesses the feasibility of contributions and finds out where and how to obtain the required resources.
6) *Monitor/evaluator*: evaluates the relevance of the contributions being made and the extent to which the team is meeting its objectives.
7) *Team Worker*: maintains the social cohesion of the group and the discussion process by joking and supporting others.
8) *Completer/finisher*: looks for conclusions and tries to get things done.

The reason for considering such a model is to allow you to think about your group, and how the people fit in.

> To Practise 3.2: Draw a grid with these *roles* along one axis, and the members of your group along the other. Consider which role characteristics each of your team display, adding 'ticks' in the appropriate squares to produce a team profile.

It is worthwhile taking another such grid into your next few meetings and filling it out using actual observations, and then comparing it to your original guesses; some of your team may surprise you.

> To Practise 3.3: What do you consider to be the most important three roles; and which do you personally fill best, and most often (not necessarily the same answer)?

If you have trouble choosing the most important three, then you are well on the way to a good understanding of the problem. The established answer is that all eight roles are equally important since the long-term success of a group depends upon each being filled by someone – lose one, and you lose the effectiveness of the group.

There remains the question, though, as to which role you, as manager, *should* fill. Commonly, the manager assumes the role of the Chair simply because that is conventionally the position of authority. The effect of this, however, can be to stifle contributions from the team who defer to your position (as manager *and* as Chair). The role of Chair is actually a fairly mechanical one: he/she must keep the meeting moving forward, ensure that all have the chance to speak, remind the meeting of necessary points of procedure. These are skills which all of the team could learn/perform, so give them the chance. If the most visible symbol of authority in a meeting (the Chair) is passed regularly around the group, then each will feel part of that authority (thus raising self-esteem), be more likely to contribute ideas in the future (because each has spoken in the past), and be less inclined to disrupt a meeting (because each has to control one in the future). Thus the role of Chair is one you can assign to very positive effect. Of course, if things do go wrong, you can step in (to support the Chair) – and this should be viewed as part of the supportive learning you are encouraging.

So what role should you fill? There are two answers. Once you have decide upon your real strengths, play them. These may actually be the reason for your promotion in the first place,so why deny them to the group now that you are manager? Of course, this is a further reason for abdicating the Chair. The other answer stems from your role as Planner (see chapter 1): since you have to take a longer-term view, and since you have access to information concerning the broader picture within the company, you are best placed (of all the team members) to fill the role of *company worker*. It is a role which needs to be filled; you are best placed to fill it; so fill it.

What do you need to look for in the team grids? Firstly, you need to check that each person actually does contribute something. If not, then he/she must be given something to do to 'kick-start' them into activity. This could simply be a piece of research ('find out about ...') which has to be presented to the next meeting making him/her an expert. Alternatively, you could actively elicit contributions or suggestions from that person during the meetings. You judge what to do.

Secondly, you should check that all the roles are actually filled within your group. If you perceive a deficiency in the group roles, you must devise a plan to get it filled – you are in charge, you have to do something about it or the group performance will suffer. In terms of moving the group forward, the *shaper* and the *monitor/evaluator* have the most positive effect in that they both analyse and review the state of the discussion and so refocus the team's deliberations. These are roles you can foster in others by asking them to fill them in the meeting. So if Colin has just spoken for too long, ask him to summarize his view; if the discussion has lost track, ask Clare to review the position.

> *To Practise 3.4:* Thinking about yourself again, rank the eight roles according to your current habits (i.e. how often you fill each role). *Write this down* in your notebook.

However, there is another perspective on this. How can you develop yourself to be an optimal team member? Given that, in your working life, you will have to function in a large variety of different groups with different compositions and different practices, how can you possibly prepare to be useful in them all? I advocate a two-pronged attack: choose your strength and play it, choose your weakness and eliminate it. The reason for the first prong is obvious; for the second, the reason is as follows. The best person to have on a team is someone who observes how the team is working and then adapts to fill the deficient roles. Thus the best team member is the one who is flexible enough to fill all roles – and if you are lacking any of these roles, you should practise them.

> *To Practise 3.5:* Choose role number six (no cheating) from your ranking in the previous question (not too ambitious to begin with) and consider precisely what such a person does to fill that role. If you are puzzled, look back at your grids of your team and decide what made you attribute that role to someone else. At the next few meetings, imitate.

If you are helping your own team to follow a similar path of self development the message is simple: *each person is responsible for ensuring that all roles are filled in any group activity.*

3.3 Group Development

The role analysis of group work deals primarily with established groups. If you are starting out with a fresh group, or with a group that has gone stale, it is worthwhile looking at how groups evolve. It is common to view the development of a group as having four stages:

FORMING
STORMING
NORMING
PERFORMING

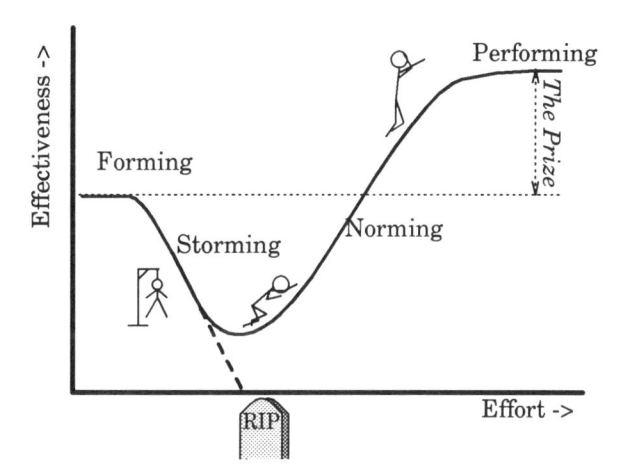

Forming is the stage when the group first comes together. Everybody is very polite and very dull. Conflict is seldom voiced directly, and what is voiced is mainly personal and definitely destructive. Since the grouping is new, the individuals will be guarded in their own opinions and generally reserved. This is particularly so in terms of the more nervous and/or subordinate members who may never recover. The group tends to defer to a large extent to those who emerge as leaders (poor fools!).

Storming is the next stage, when all Hell breaks loose and the leaders are lynched. Factions form, personalities clash, no one concedes a single point without first fighting tooth and nail. Most importantly, very little communication occurs since no one is listening and some are still unwilling to talk openly. True, this image of the battle ground may seem a little extreme for the groups to which you belong – but if you look beneath the veil of civility, at the sarcasm, invective and innuendo, perhaps then the picture comes more into focus. Unfortunately, some groups never pass beyond the Storming phase and are lost to us all.

Then comes the Norming. At this stage the sub-groups begin to recognize the merits of working together and the in-fighting subsides. Since a new spirit of co-operation is evident, members begin to feel secure in expressing their own view points and these are discussed openly with the whole group. The most significant improvement is that people start to listen to each other. Work methods become established and recognized by everyone.

And finally: Performing. This is the culmination, when the group has settled on a system which allows free and frank exchange of views and a high degree of support by the group for each other and its own decisions.

In terms of performance, the group starts at a level slightly below the sum of the individuals' levels and then drops abruptly to its nadir until it climbs during Norming to a new level of Performing which is (hopefully) well above the original. It is this elevated level of performance which is the main justification for using the group process rather than a simple group of staff.

> *To Practise 3.6:* Mark where you believe your group to be on the effectiveness curve.

The group process is achieved through a series of changes which occur as a group of individuals form into a cohesive and effective operating unit. The graph above has 'effort' on the bottom axis because this is the important quantity. Given sufficient time, some groups (using common sense) apply sufficient effort to bring about their eventual evolution into an effective, performing, co-operative group. Given sensible emphasis, the group process may be directly managed and specific effort applied early on, so that the evolution is accelerated and Performing is achieved far earlier. Thus a little time spent in managing the group process will save the group much more time in the future.

3.4 Group Skills

There are two main sets of skills which a group needs to acquire:

- Managerial Skills
- Interpersonal Skills

and the acceleration of the group process is simply the accelerated acquisition of these.

As a self-managing unit, a group can undertake most of the functions of a manager – collectively. For instance, meetings must be organized, budgets decided, strategic planning undertaken, goals set, performance monitored, reviews scheduled, etc. It is increasingly recognized that it is a fallacy to expect an individual (like you) to suddenly assume managerial responsibility without assistance; in the group this is even more true. Even if there are practised managers in the group, they must first agree on a method, and then convince and train the remainder.

Commonly, a new group needs to relearn basic manners and people-management skills. Again, think of that self-opinionated, cantankerous loud-mouth; he/she should learn good manners, and the group must learn to enforce these manners without destructive confrontation.

It is common practice in accelerating group development to appoint, and if necessary to train, a 'group facilitator'. The role of this person is to draw the group's attention continually to the group process and to suggest structures and practices to support and enhance the group skills. This must be only a short-term training strategy, however, since the existence of a single facilitator may prevent the group from assuming collective responsibility for the group process.

The aim of any group should be that *facilitation is performed by every member equally and constantly*. If this responsibility is recognized and undertaken from the beginning by all, then the Storming phase may be avoided and the group development will pass straight into Norming.

You, as manager, ultimately have the responsibility for making sure that the group process is maintained. The aim is that the group will one day undertake this itself, but, particularly in initial formation, you will need to intervene directly. This is not necessarily bad since the team then has an authoritative role model for self maintenance. The following is a set of suggestions which may help. They are offered as suggestions, no more; a group will work towards its own practices and norms.

Brainstorming

Particularly for the generation of new idea, but also for sharing opinions, brainstorming is a simple direct procedure. The idea of brainstorming is that the group spends a short, specified amount of time generating ideas *without any comment*, followed by a longer period in which these are analysed. The important point is that no idea is too wild or too bizarre.

A mild brainstorm

First, establish the question: why are you studying this course, what is the market place for this product, how might Machiavelli have utilized market forces? Then for (say) three minutes, someone writes on the board or flipchart, each and every suggestion. No one is allowed to comment upon the suggestion during the brainstorming – especially there must be no criticism. After the allotted time, the group then examines each idea in turn and *tries to build upon it*. Having examined each idea in terms of pros and cons, the group then decides upon a course of action.

When introducing this technique to a group for the first time, it is worth emphasizing that it is used extensively within industry as a means of generating innovation and creativity.

Focus
The two basic focuses should be the *group* and the *task*.

If something is to be decided, it is the group that decides it. If there is a problem, the group solves it. If a member is performing badly, it is the group who asks for change.

If individual conflicts arise, review them in terms of the task. If there is initially a lack of structure and purpose in the deliberations, impose both in terms of the task. If there are disputes between alternative courses of action, negotiate in terms of the task.

Clarification
In any project management, the clarity of the specification is of paramount importance – in group work it is exponentially so. Suppose that there is a four in five chance of an individual understanding the task correctly (which is very high). If there are eight members in the group then the chance of the group all working with the same, correct understanding of the task is less than one in five. And the same reasoning holds for every decision and action taken throughout the life of the group.

It is the first responsibility of the group to clarify its own task, and to record this understanding so that it can be constantly seen. This *mission statement* may be revised or replaced, but it should always act as a focus for the group's deliberations and actions.

The written record
Often a decision which is not recorded will become clouded and have to be re-discussed. This can be avoided simply by recording on a large display (where the group can clearly see) each decision as it is made. This has the further advantage that each decision must be expressed in a clear and concise

form which ensures that it is clarified. This should be recorded and distributed after the meeting.

The mouse
In any group, there is always the quiet one in the corner who says little. That individual is *the* most under-utilized resource in the whole group, and so represents the best return for minimal effort by the group as a whole. It is the responsibility of that individual to speak out and contribute. It is the responsibility of the group to encourage and develop that person, to include him/her in the discussion and actions, and to provide positive reinforcement each time the mouse squeaks.

The loud-mouth
In any group, there is always a dominant member whose opinions form a disproportionate share of the discussion. It is the responsibility of each individual to consider whether he/she is that person. It is the responsibility of the group to ask whether the loud-mouth might like to summarize briefly, and then ask for other views.

> *To Practise 3.7:* Select from your team the winners of the previous two categories (include yourself in the nominations). Decide, now, how you are going to deal with this.

Feedback (negative)
All criticism must be neutral: focused on the task and not the personality. So rather than calling Arnold an innumerate moron, point out the error and offer him a calculator. It is wise to adopt the policy of giving feedback frequently, especially for small things – this can be couched as mutual coaching, and it reduces the destructive impact of criticism when things go badly wrong.

Every criticism must be accompanied by a positive suggestion for improvement

Feedback (positive)
If anyone does something well, praise it. Not only does this reinforce commendable actions, but it also mollifies the negative feedback which may come later. Progress in the task should be emphasized.

Handling failure

The long-term success of a group depends upon how it deals with failure. It is a very common tendency to brush off failure and to get on with the next stage with no more than a mention – it is a very foolish tendency. Any failure should be explored by the group. This is not to attribute blame (for that is shared by the whole group since an individual only acts with delegated responsibility), but rather to examine the causes and to devise a mechanism which either monitors against or prevents repetition. A mistake should only happen once if it is treated correctly.

One practice which is particularly useful is to delegate the agreed solution to the individual or sub-group who made the original error. This allows the group to demonstrate its continuing trust, and the penitent to make amends.

> *To Practise 3.8:* Pick your team's last minor shortcoming and devise a plan to ensure that it does not happen again. If possible ask those involved – but make your intention clear from the beginning of the discussion.

Handling deadlock

If two opposing points of view are held in the group then some action must be taken. Several possible strategies exist. Each faction could debate from the other faction's viewpoint in order to understand it better. Common ground could be emphasized, and the differences viewed for a possible middle or alternative strategy. Each view should be debated in the light of the original task. But, firstly, the group should decide how much time the debate actually merits and then guillotine it after that time – then, if the issue is not critical, toss a coin.

Accepting group decisions

It is better to accept a decision with which one personally disagrees and to get the thing done, rather than to keep arguing the point again, again and again. You just learn to accept things because it is a group – and acceptance is the only way to move things forward. If you still feel that the wrong decision has been taken, learn that next time you must present your own point of view more effectively.

Sign posting

As each small point is discussed, the larger picture can be obscured. Thus it is useful to remind the group frequently: this is where we came from, this is where we are, this is where we should be going. Actually doing the sign-posting is also a marvellous way of following the flow of a meeting since you have to concentrate upon extracting the essential message from each contribution and evaluating that in terms of its relevance to the task. It also helps you to phrase your own contributions in a more succinct manner.

> *To Practise 3.9:* At your next meeting, take minutes of the proceedings for yourself in the form of sub-sentence summaries of each contribution, emphasizing its relevance to the task.

Avoid single solutions
First ideas are not always best. For any given problem, the group should generate alternatives, evaluate these in terms of the task, pick one and implement it. But, most importantly, they must also monitor the outcome, schedule a review and be prepared to change the plan.

Active communication
Communication is the responsibility of both the speaker and the listener. The speaker must actively seek to express ideas in a clear and concise manner – the listener must actively seek to understand what has been said and to ask for clarification if unsure. Finally, both parties must be sure that the ideas have been correctly communicated, perhaps by the listener summarizing what was said in a different way.

Discussion and Learning
One of the best learning aspects of a group is that is allows people to bounce ideas around in a non-critical environment and so allows people to talk through ideas (even if they seem 'silly'). Often, a group can throw up a set of seemingly unconnected thoughts which can be synthesized into a valid and novel plan. Further, the mere act of talking through points will clarify and possibly improve (through mutual help) the general understanding of the problem.

Co-dominance
Because the situation is constantly shifting, and because each individual has a unique contribution, there must be no rigid hierarchy within the group. If a hierarchy exists, it will cause inertia and reduce the group's flexibility to respond to change. The aim should be 'co-dominance': where each person assumes authority when appropriate and relinquishes it immediately after. If you need to be more formal, then formally ask: 'Who should lead now?'

Finishing each meeting
No group discussion should be terminated without a clear and agreed plan of action to take the work forward. Preferably, this should include a list of actions, responsibilities, and dates. Even if the agreed action is inaction, there should be a designated date for the next review.

> *To Practise 3.10:* Add two suggestions of your own: what practices have you observed which make a group work well?

3.5 Putting this into Practice

Groups are like relationships – you have to work at them. In the work place, they constitute an important unit of activity but one whose support needs are only recently becoming understood. By making the group itself responsible for its own support, the responsibility becomes an accelerator for the group process. What is vital is that the need to manage the group process is recognized and explicitly dealt with by the group. Time and resources must be allocated to this by the group and by you (as manager); the group process must be planned, monitored and reviewed just like any other managed process.

As a manager, you hope to use the group process to increase the effectiveness of your team. Unfortunately, you yourself may be the main restriction upon the team development since, unless you are actually willing to allow them to make contributions and even to make decisions, they will not see any point in making the effort. The simple rule is that you should accept any group decision unless it has obviously detrimental consequences. This is practically a contradiction, since if the consequences are obviously bad then the group will not make that decision – unless you have not provided them with sufficient learning or information.

Your objective is to enable your team to manage its own activity. Ultimately, you will pass the authority to them, allowing you to focus upon the wider issues of your job as manager. One approach is to make group work an issue: give a presentation to your team about the value of working together. If you do not believe that there is sufficient material in this chapter alone, read further and observe. To start the team off, you need to give them some clear initial goals and possibly some training (your personnel department might help with this). Note: if there is a training course, you must attend with the rest of the team otherwise they will merely return with a clearer understanding of your ignorance. One possible starting point for team work, is to apply Quality – as will be explained in chapter 7.

If you want a gentler beginning, start simply by calling 'strategy' meetings on a regular basis. This allows you to communicate the current position and direction with the team (making them feel less in the dark) and to ask for their input. Do not be put off by initial silence – sit with it until someone is embarrassed enough to break it for you. If any of their initial suggestions has a non-detrimental outcome (not necessarily good, merely non-bad) then get the whole team to develop it and get it implemented. A quick, tangible sign that you are willing to act will engender greater co-operation in the future.

When assigning future tasks, ask the whole team whether anyone has particular knowledge – and assign that person as a 'tutor' to help someone else to whom you actually assign the task. Make this interaction as informal as possible, but check regularly that it is occurring. The more tasks which can be given to small teams, the more genuine co-operation will be created.

Buy plenty of flip-charts or writing boards so that these are readily available and start using them to clarify your own presentations and for recording the progress/ideas in your team meetings. Writing on the board is another role similar to (or replacing that of) the Chair which you could assign to others in your team.

For you, it is again a case of deliberately forcing yourself to spend time and effort observing and applying new ideas to help the group work forward. *Watch the Manager* can be played at any group meeting you attend. Firstly, play with the 'role grids' and observe specific actions by which these roles are achieved. This will help you to emulate the good and to avoid the destructive. Secondly, start choosing one of the above facilitation techniques and applying it in the next meeting; a different technique for each meeting. Thus your notebook should contain an entry before each meeting designating your selected technique, and an entry after detailing the lessons from your experience.

Summary of Team-work

Who should I be today?

- Company Worker
- Chair
- Shaper
- Ideas Person
- Resource investigator
- Monitor/evaluator
- Team Worker
- Completer/finisher

Every team member should act as a facilitator

Every team member should adapt to fill missing roles

Which should I try today?

- Brainstorming
- Focus (group/task)
- Clarification
- Written Record
- Mouse trap
- Silencer
- Feedback
- Handling failure (sob!)
- Handling deadlock
- Accepting group decisions
- Sign Posting
- Active Communication
- Discussion and Learning
- Co-dominance
- Finishing well
- -
- -

{ add your two here

Chapter: 4
Time Management

Tempus edax rerum – time, the devourer of affairs
(Ovid)

Time passes, quickly. Time management is about controlling the use of your most valuable (and undervalued) resource. As you assume managerial responsibility, you find that there are many extra demands made upon your time and many more reasons for husbanding it for longer-term affairs. The absence of time management is characterized by last-minute rushes to meet dead-lines, meetings which are either double-booked or achieve nothing, days which seem somehow to slip unproductively by, crises which loom unexpectedly from nowhere. This sort of environment leads to inordinate stress and degradation of performance. It must be stopped. Consider these two questions. What would happen if you spent company money with as few safeguards as you spend company time? When was the last time *you* scheduled a review of your own time allocation?

Poor time management is often a symptom of over-confidence. In many cases, techniques which used to work with small projects and workloads are simply reused with large ones. But inefficiencies which were insignificant in the small are ludicrous in the large. You cannot drive a motor-bike like a bicycle, nor can you manage a supermarket chain like a market stall. The demands, the problems, and the pay-offs for increased efficiency are all larger as your responsibility grows; you must learn to apply proper techniques or be bettered by those who do.

One of the main problems with training (especially self-training) in time management is that few people recognize the need. Most managers have experience of deadlines and schedules, and there is always the ubiquitous appointments diary; thus most believe that they have a sufficient grasp of time management and so that this chapter is superfluous. Read on and weep.

4.1 Watch the Time

As a first perspective on time management, consider the three *'Eff'* words [*concise OED*]:

- Effective: having a definite or desired effect
- Efficient: productive with minimum waste or effort
- Effortless: seemingly without effort; natural, easy

Time management is about mastering the *'Eff'* words, making them apply to you and your daily routines.

> *To Practise 4.1:* Try to answer the following questions:
> Does the day sometimes disappear?   Yes/No
> Do you rush to meet deadlines?   Yes/No
> What are your three main activities?   (in notebook)
> What proportion of time is spent on them?   ____%
> Are their end-dates known/practical?   Yes/No Yes/No

> *To Practise 4.2:* Suppose you have a lot to do at work at the moment. Things are really busy. If your manager comes in and asks you to do this extra little job by next Friday, would you say NO? If so, could you discuss/explain/justify that reaction?

Time management has many facets. Most managers recognize a few, but few recognize them all. There is the simple concept of keeping a well-ordered diary and the related idea of planned activity. But time management goes far beyond these. Time management is a tool which gives *you* control. It allows you to achieve a systematic ordering of your influence on events, and it underpins many other managerial skills such as effective delegation and project planning.

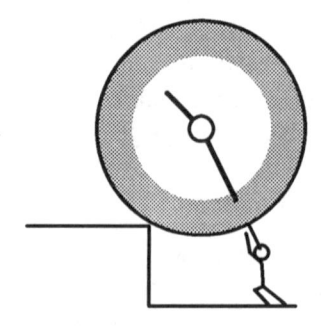

Time management enables you to:
- eliminate wastage
- be prepared for meetings
- refuse excessive workloads
- monitor project progress
- allocate time appropriate to a task's importance
- ensure that long-term projects are not neglected
- plan each day efficiently and each week effectively

and to do so simply with a little self-discipline.

What this chapter is advocating is the adoption of certain practices which will give you greater control over the use and allocation of your primary resource: *time*. Before we start on the future, it is worth considering the present. This involves the simple task of keeping a note of how you spend your time for a suitable period: at least a day (if it is representative), longer if possible. All you have to do is to complete a simple table like the one shown below. Carry it around with you and fill in a row for each change of activity (including the trivial. such as going for a cup of coffee).

Activity	Start	Finish	Comments

Since time management is a management process just like any other, it must be planned, monitored and regularly reviewed. This takes you far beyond simply recording appointments, to a complete and comprehensive review of all your work practices. In the following sections, we will examine the basic methods and functions of time management so that you can adapt them to your own requirements. This will actually involve some serious monitoring and thought about your current use of time; if this cannot be fitted in right now – ask yourself: why not?

> *To Practise 4.3:* Keep a log and allocate time (start as you mean to go on) to review this log.

4.2 Waste Disposal

We are not looking in this section to create new categories of work to enhance efficiency (that comes later) but simply to eliminate waste in your current practice. First of all, let us consider how much your time is actually worth. To start with, consider your gross salary. As a rough approximation, there are 1600 hours in a working year (without overtime).

> *To Practise 4.4:* Work out your gross salary per hour.

Of course from the company's point of view, you cost a lot more than your salary. To take into account taxation, health-care, pensions and the cost of furniture, electronic equipment, floor space, etc; you should triple the simple salary costs. Finally, you should add a factor for the profit the company hopes to make by employing you.

> *To Practise 4.5:* Work out how much your hour is worth to the company. How much time does a pound (dollar) buy?

Now that we have this in a little better perspective, let us see exactly what you are doing to merit this money. Your judgement might be sharpened if you considered whether you would be prepared to pay someone else as much, out of your own pocket, for doing the same work. In your time log, identify periods of time which might not be worth as much as you received.

There are various sources of waste. The most common are social: telephone calls, friends dropping by, conversations around the coffee machine. It would be foolish to eliminate all non work-related activity (we all need a break) but if it is a choice between chatting to Arnold in the afternoon and meeting the next deadline ... . Your time log will show you if this is a problem and you might like to do something about it before your manager does.

Another source of waste relates to the start-up periods associated with changes between activities. Not only do you normally have to physically move paper or equipment around, but it takes a little while to 'change gear'. Thus it is wise to group similar tasks together. Do the mail once, and completely. Tackle a few tasks each day for a long time, rather than many tasks for a short time. Put interruptions into a pending tray, rather than deal with them in the middle of something else. Use your time log to identify any ineffective, short jobs which could be better grouped and tackled together. In some cases, you can decide upon a simple habit (non-urgent letters on Tuesday morning) which controls your in-tray *and* allows other people to plan their activities around your routine.

As a point of principle, remember that you are the manager and *you* should be managing the use of your time; not every Tom, Dick or Harriet who walks into your office demanding attention. Even your own team should be made to realize that your time is valuable and that if they need it, they should use it without causing disruption. As manager, you need to be available, but few problems are so urgent that they cannot be allocated a convenient time in the near future. Thus you strike a deal.

The next major time waster is the jobs you enjoy. In your time log, look at each work activity and decide objectively how much time each was *worth* and compare that with the time you actually spent on it. An afternoon passed polishing an internal memo into a Pulitzer prize-winning piece of provocative prose is waste; an hour spent debating the leaving present of a colleague is waste; a minute spent sorting out the paper-clips is waste (unless relaxation). This type of activity will be reduced naturally by managing your own time since you will not allocate time to the trivial. Specifically, if you have a task to do, *decide beforehand how long it should take and work to that deadline* – then move on to the next task.

On the other hand, a major time waster is the jobs you loath. Procrastination devours huge tracts of time simply because the necessary (unpleasant) work is replaced with time-filling (unnecessary) activity. The loathsome work slips until it has to be tackled too late and so is done poorly. In fact, if the time you spent procrastinating had been devoted to creating better ways of achieving the same end, it might actually have been productive. Check your log to see if any tasks are being delayed simply because they are dull or difficult.

> *To Practise 4.6:* Identify your favourite and your least loved tasks. For the former, consider how it could be shortened (decreasing your indulgence); for the latter, consider changing it to make it more enjoyable – any job can be reviewed and changed.

4.3 Doing the Work of Others

Having considered what is complete waste, we now turn to what is merely inappropriate. Often it is simpler to do the job yourself. Using the stamp machine to frank your own letters ensures they leave by the next post; writing the missing summary in the latest progress report from your junior is more pleasant than sending it back (and it lets you choose the emphasis). Rubbish!

Large gains can be made by assigning secretarial duties to secretaries; they regularly catch the next post, they type a lot faster than you. Your subordinate should be told about the missing section and told how (and why) to slant it. If you have a task which could be done by a subordinate, use the next occasion to start training him/her to do it instead of doing it yourself – you will need to spend some time monitoring the task thereafter but far less than in doing it yourself.

A major impact upon your work can be the tendency to help others with theirs. Now, in the spirit of an open and harmonious work environment it is obviously desirable that you should be willing to help out – but check your work log and decide how much time you spend on your own work and how much you spend on others'. For instance, if you spend a morning checking the grammar and spelling in the publicity material relating to your last project, then that is waste. The Documentation group should do the proof-reading, that is their job, they are better at it than you; you should be checking the technical details about which you have special knowledge.

The remaining problem is your manager. Consider what periods in your work log were used to perform tasks that your manager either repeated or simply negated by ignoring your work or redefining the task too late. Making your manager efficient is a very difficult task, but where it impinges upon your work and performance you must take the bull by the horns and confront the issue. Managing your manager may seem a long way from time management but no one impacts upon your use of time more than your immediate superior. If a task is ill defined – seek clarification ('is that a one-page summary or a ten-page report?'). If seemingly random alterations are requested in your deliverables, ask for the reasons and next time clarify these and similar points at the beginning. If the manager is difficult, try writing a small specification for each task before beginning it and have it agreed. While you cannot hold your manager to this contract if he/she has a change of mind, it will at least cause him/her to consider the issues early on, before you waste your time on false assumptions.

> *To Practise 4.7:* A difficult question. Of the three groups of people: those above you, beside you and below you – which affect your time management the most adversely? Pick that group, and *write* a three-point strategy for addressing the problem during the next month.

4.4 External Appointments

The next stage of time management is to start taking control of your time. The first problem is appointments. Start with a simple appointments diary. In this book you will have (or at least should have) a complete list of all your known appointments for the foreseeable future. If you have omitted your regular ones (since you remember them anyway) add them now.

Your appointments constitute your interaction with other people; they are the agreed interface between your activities and those of others; they are determined by external obligation. They often fill the diary. Now, be ruthless – and eliminate the unnecessary. There may be committees where you cannot productively contribute or where a subordinate might be (better) able to participate. There may be long lunches which could be better run as short conference calls. There may be interviews which last three times as long as necessary because they are scheduled for a whole hour. Eliminate the wastage starting today.

'Be ruthless ...' *Grrrrr!*

The next stage is to add to your diary lists of other, personal activities which will enhance your use of the available time.

> *To Practise 4.8:* Consider: what is the most important type of activity to add to your diary? No – stop reading for a moment and really consider.

The single most important type of activity is that which will save you time. Allocate time to save time, a stitch in time saves days. And most importantly of all, always allocate time to managing time, at least five minutes each and every day.

For each appointment left in the diary (after you were ruthless), consider what actions you might take to ensure that no time is wasted. *Plan to avoid unnecessary work by being prepared.* This is a practical aspect of being a Planner. Thus, if you are going to a meeting where you will be asked to comment on some report, allocate time to read it, so avoiding delays in the meeting and increasing your chances of making the right decision first time.

Consider what actions need to be taken *before* and what actions must be taken *after* to follow-up. Even if the latter are unclear before the event, you must still allocate time to review the outcome and to plan the resulting actions. Simply mark in your diary a block of time to do this and, when the time comes – do it.

4.5 Scheduling Work

The most daunting external appointments are deadlines: often, the hand-over of deliverables. Do you leave the work too late? Is there commonly a final panic towards the end? Are the last few hectic hours often marred by errors? If so, use time management.

The basic idea is that your management of your own deadlines should be achieved with exactly the same techniques you would use in a large project:

1) check the specification – are you sure that you have agreed on precisely what is required and by when?

2) break the task down into small sections so that you can estimate the time needed for each, and monitor progress

3) schedule reviews of your progress (e.g. after each sub-task) so that you can respond quickly to difficulties

Just to illustrate the first point. If I told you to 'get the report ready for me for next month' would you interpret that to mean: 1) by midnight on the last day of next month, 2) by 8am on the first day of next month, 3) any time at all next month (I don't care), or 4) any time next month but sooner rather than later (I was giving you scope to show your prowess)? If you answered any of these, then *wrong – no prize*. I have to present that report at the beginning of next month ('ready *for me* for next month') and common sense should tell you that I need it at least a week beforehand to digest it. You should check and double check your job specifications (especially the verbal ones) for ambiguities, and plain inarticulateness.

Like most management ideas, the management of time is common sense. Some people, however, refute it because in practice they find that it merely shows the lack of time for a project which must be done anyway. This is plain daft! If simple project planning and time management show that the task cannot be done, then it will not be done – but by knowing at the start, you have a chance to do something about it.

An impossible deadline affects not only your success but also that of others. Suppose a product release is scheduled too soon because you agreed to deliver too early. Marketing excite the customers by proving that they need (and cannot live without) the new product – and it does not arrive. The customers are dissatisfied or even lost, the competition has advanced warning, and all because you agreed to do the impossible.

You can avoid this type of problem. By practising time management, you will always have a clear understanding of how you spend your time and what time is unallocated. If a new task is thrust upon you, you can estimate whether it is practical. The project planning tells you how much time is needed and the time management tells you how much time is available.

There are four ways to deal with impossible deadlines:

1) Get the deadline extended

2) Scream for more resources

3) Redefine the project to something practical in the available time

4) Start working but state the position clearly to your boss (*and* his/her boss)

If this simple approach seems unrealistic, consider the alternative. If you have an imposed, but unobtainable, deadline and you accept it, then the outcome is *your* assured failure. Of course, there is a fifth option: move to a company with realism.

One defence tactic is to present your superior with a list of your current obligations indicating what impact the new task will have on these, and ask him/her to assign the priorities: 'We cannot do them all – which should we let slip?' Another tactic is to keep a data base of your time estimates and the actual time taken by each task. This will quickly develop into a source of valuable data and increase the accuracy of your planning predictions.

There is no reason why you should respond only to externally imposed deadlines. The slightly shoddy product which you hand over after the last-minute rush (and normally have returned for correction the following week) could easily have been polished if only an extra day had been available – so move your personal deadline forward and allow yourself the luxury of leisured review before the product is shipped. Taking this a step further, the same sort of review might be applied to the product at each stage of its development so that errors and rework time are reduced. Thus by allocating time to quality review, you save time in rework; and this is all part of project planning supported and monitored by your time management.

Finally, for each activity you should estimate how much time it is worth and allocate only that amount. This critical appraisal may even suggest a different approach or method so that the time matches the task's importance. Beware of perfection, it takes too long; allocate sufficient time to achieve 'fitness for purpose' – then stop.

> *To Practise 4.9:* Consider your tightest deadline. Is it practical? Will it be a 'quality' job you would be proud to show to a potential employer? Your manager intends to tell you *tomorrow* that delivery is needed earlier than agreed (in 70% of the remaining time) – plan your response.

4.6 Looking Further Afield

Your time management also affects other people, particularly your subordinates. Planning projects means not only allocating your time but also distributing tasks; and this should be done in the same planned, monitored and reviewed manner as your own scheduling.

Any delegated task should be specified with an (agreed) end date. As a manager, you are responsible for ensuring that the tasks allocated to your subordinates are completed successfully. Thus you should ensure that each task is concluded with a deliverable (for instance, a memo to confirm completion) – you make an entry in your diary to check that this has arrived. Thus, if you agree the task for Tuesday, Wednesday should have an entry in your diary to check upon the deliverable. This simple device allows you to monitor progress and to initiate action as necessary.

There are many long-term objectives which you (as a *great* manager) must achieve, particularly with regard to the development, support and motivation of your team. Long-term objectives have the problem of being important but not urgent; they have no deadlines, they are distant and remote. For this reason, it is all too easy to ignore them in favour of the urgent and immediate. Clearly a balance must be struck.

The beauty of time management is that the balance can be decided objectively (without influence from immediate deadlines) and self-imposed through the use of the diary. Simply, a manager might decide that one hour a week should be devoted to personnel issues and so allocate a regular block of time to that activity. Of course if the office is on fire, or World War III is declared, the manager may have to re-allocate this time in a particular week – but barring such crises, this time should then become sacrosanct and always applied to the same, designated purpose.

Similarly, time may be allocated to staff development and training. So if one afternoon a month is deemed to be a suitable allocation, simply designate the second Thursday (say) of each month and delegate the choice of speakers. The actual time spent in managing this sort of long-term objective is small, but without that deliberate planning it will not be achieved.

Once you have implemented time management, it is worth using some of that control to augment your own career. Some quiet weekend, you should sketch out your own long-term objectives and plan a route to them. As you would any long-term objective, allocate time to the necessary sub-tasks and monitor your progress. If you do not plan where you want to go, you are unlikely to get there.

> *To Practise 4.10:* Seriously, where *do* you want to be in three years time? To achieve that, what must you have achieved in the next two years? What steps can you take this coming year to make this more likely?

4.7 A Parenthesis on Stress

Stress is one of those taboo topics. Everyone knows that it is a potential problem, but no one wants to talk about it and no one readily admits to suffering from it. The normal reason for this reticence is that to admit to stress is thought to be an admission that one cannot cope – whereas, in reality, the first step to coping with stress is to admit to it. This section may not apply to you but you should read it in case it contains some advice for a friend.

If work-related stress is causing you to be impotent or frigid, to suffer from compulsive eating or anorexia, to fail to sleep (no, one hour is not enough) or to be found after midnight chasing sheep into railway tunnels – then the best use of your time would be to put down this book, pick up the phone book, and call a doctor: you need professional help.

If work-related stress is causing you to be irritable, to drop things, to twitch, to hate getting up in the morning, to long for a transport strike, or generally to be very unhappy about life, the universe, and everything – then you need to take stock of your predicament.

Quite frankly, the answer to your problems may not lie in your work at all; an adventure holiday, or a good dose of flu, might be all you need to gain a new outlook and a new fondness for your current routine. However, much work-related stress is caused by the pressure of imposed schedules, of too heavy and unreasonable demands; time management is one way to gain a sense of perspective.

If you take control of your time, and objectively review your schedules and commitments, you can establish what is possible. Then, having thought it through, you can look at the rest of your work load and smile: it cannot be done, so why make yourself ill by trying? Once the problem is established, you can work towards a solution in terms of prioritizing some tasks, jettisoning others, reducing the scope of still others, and getting help with the rest. Since you have decided (and can show) that the work cannot all be done, there is no loss to the company in your making arrangements accordingly – indeed an early warning is the best outcome the company deserves. If your manager complains vociferously, he/she is probably just trying to 'motivate' you to work harder – smile, and explain the problem again. Plan the use of your time and enjoy the work – you will get more done this way than by aiming at the impractical.

Often, stress is simply a case of too narrow a perspective. If you have trouble coming to terms with your own misfortune consider that of others. For instance, St Lawrence was put to death (in the year 258 AD) by being roasted over a gridiron. During this torture he remarked: 'see I am done enough on this side, turn me over and cook the other'. Later he added: 'manduca iam coctum est' (he was an educated gent) which means: 'eat up, it's done already'. Are your problems worse that this? Can you maintain a sense of humour?

Another example is that of St Cecilia (2-3 century AD) who refused to renounce her faith in front of the Roman Prefect Almachius. He suffered 'exceeding wroth' and ordered her to be boiled in a bath of oil. This, however, did not kill Cecilia and so an axeman was called to remove her head (while still in the bath). Unfortunately, the law stated that a beheader was only allowed three blows, and three blundered blows later the head was still on (or at least partially) and she lingered. If you feel no pity for Cecilia, spare a thought for Almachius who could not even organize a decent execution and, for the next three days, had to put up with this half-fried woman sitting in his bath, bleeding over the carpet and bequeathing all her wealth to the poor. Surely your project is not as poorly organized as his? Will your incompetence still be remarked upon after seventeen hundred years?

And if any reader thinks that this is too flippant a treatment of such an important subject, please remember: you have to laugh – that is the first step to dealing with stress.

One final cause of stress is unrelieved monotony. Under pressure, it is too easy to focus exclusively on your problems, and never to take a break. You must.

> *To Practise 4.11:* Do something totally different and unexpected this evening.

4.8 A Total Review

The final stage of time management is a total review of your current work practices. Once you have your diary under control and have been watching your time for a while, it will become obvious that things are not quite as they might be. By looking critically at what you actually spend your time doing, you can start to re-distribute that time to optimal use. Again, time is a resource which must be managed.

The first step is to decide what is the aim of your job. One place to look might be in your job description or your annual appraisal – but in case neither of these are useful, try it this way. Brainstorm on the question: what does the company pay you for?

One of your key functions is probably that of manager. You have responsibility for ensuring that your team fulfil their functions – and that brings you back to chapter 1. Another key function is found in what you actually produce (whether it is a service or a tangible product) and you need to decide how important that is to the aims of the company. This, of course, leads you to an alternative question: what is the company for, and how do you affect the outcome? All this is very abstract, so if you do not arrive at anything concrete settle for an old stand-by: what do you do that no one else does and which must be done?

> *To Practise 4.12:* Write down (in your notebook) at most three sentences which describe the primary functions of your current position.

Once you have a clear(er) idea of what is actually important in your job, look at how you spend your time. Start by identifying unimportant activities on which you spend large amounts of time; then look are the important activities on which you spend little; finally, devise ways of moving each task out of these categories. This is not necessarily easy, but it is extremely necessary.

Essentially, you need to estimate how much each task is worth in terms of your job functions, and allocate to it that amount of time and no more. This will involve being creative, evolving new systems, delegating some tasks (see chapter 6) and even redefining the tasks themselves. If this is the first time you have appraised your work this way, you are bound to find at least one job which simply does not need doing any more – either because someone has left the company, or because a system has changed, or because someone else duplicates the work. The main benefit, however, is the time this frees for your real work – and you will probably have to add new tasks to your list to cover any activities you have neglected.

Finally, you should look hard at the way you tackle each remaining task. For each task, try to evolve a new way of approaching it which can save your time; by evolving new ways of doing old jobs, you can end up doing far more in less time.

> *To Practise 4.13:* Take one job which currently takes a lot of your time and *write it in your notebook*. Over the next week, think about alternative ways of doing it. Ask colleagues for suggestions, ask your team. Aim to reduce your time on this task by 25%. Do not shake your head, try it.

Time management is a systematic application of common sense strategies. It requires little effort, yet it promotes efficient work practices by highlighting wastage and leads to effective use of time by focusing it on your chosen activities. Time management does not solve your problems; it reveals them, and provides a structure to implement and monitor solutions. It enables you to take control of your own time – how you use it is then up to you.

Summary of Time Management

The Purpose of Time Management is NOT

- to fill every moment with work
- to remove spontaneity
- to drive you to overtime
- to cause you stress

The Purpose of Time Management IS

- to organize your time as you want
- to eliminate wastage
- to allow you to be prepared
- to reduce stress
- to cater for long-term needs
- to make your work: EFFECTIVE, EFFICIENT, and EFFORTLESS

How to Start

- maintain a diary
- determine objectives
- match time to tasks
- each MORNING 5 mins to plan the day
- each MONDAY 15 mins to plan the week
- each MONTH 50 mins to plan the strategy

Chapter: 5
The Written Word

I write when I'm inspired, and I see to it that I'm inspired at nine o'clock every morning
(Peter De Vries)

'Sex, romance, thrills, burlesque, satire, farce ... most enjoyable.'

'Here is everything one expects from this author but thricefold and three times as entertaining as anything he has written before.'

'A wonderful tissue of outrageous coincidences and correspondences, teasing elevations of suspense and delayed climaxes.'

(reviews of *Small World* by David Lodge)

This has nothing to do with management writing. No management report will ever get such reviews. The most significant point about management writing is that it is totally different from the writing most people were taught – and if you do not recognize and understand this difference, then your management writing will always miss the mark.

Since writing is so vital a part of your work, you can easily recoup time spent on enhancing your writing skills in the time that this will save in actually writing. Thus a small effort on the process of writing itself will make you far more efficient, and make writing a pleasure rather than a chore. This chapter examines the objectives of management writing and outlines a methodical approach which will enable anyone to produce the really great works of management literature.

5.1 Management Writing

As a manager, your writing has two major roles:

- to clarify (for both writer and reader)
- to convey information

It is this deliberate, dual aim which should form the focus for all your writing activity.

Writing is the predominant means of communication within an organization. Paper is thought to be the major product of most professionals. Some estimate that up to third of managerial work-time is engaged in written communication. Thus it is absolutely vital for you as a manager to develop actively the skill of writing not only because of the time involved in writing, but also because your project's success may depend upon it. Indeed, since so much of the communication between you and more senior management occurs in writing, your whole career may depend upon its quality.

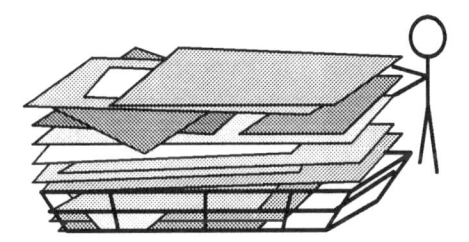

There are many uses for paper within an organization. Some are inefficient, but the power of paper must not be ignored because of that. In relation to a project, documentation provides a means to clarify and explain on-going development, and to plan the next stages. Memoranda are a simple mechanism for suggestions, instructions and general organization. The minutes of a meeting form a permanent and definitive record. Writing is a central part of any planning activity; the quality is improved since writing an explanation of the plan forces the planner to consider and explore it fully. For instance, if you habitually include a section entitled 'Methods of Monitoring', then you will force yourself to consider and solve the problems involved in tracking a project. Plans which work just 'because they do' may not; plans whose operation is explained in writing may also fail, but the review will be far quicker since the (documented) plan is thought-out and accessible to all.

Management writing has very little to do with much of the composition and literature learnt at school: the objectives are different, the audience has different needs, and the rewards can be far greater. As a manager, you write for very distinct and restricted purposes, which are best achieved through simplicity.

It is all a question of aim. A novel entertains. It forces the reader to want to know 'what happens next'. On the other hand, a management report is primarily designed to convey information. The manager's job is helped if the report is interesting, but time is short and the sooner the meat of the document is reached, the better. The novel would start: 'The dog grew ill from howling so ...'; the manager's report would start (and probably end): 'The butler killed Sir Arnold Hepplethwaite in the library with a twelve-inch carving knife'.

In school you are taught to display knowledge. The more information and argument, the more marks. In industry, it is totally different. Here the wise manager must extract only the significant information and support it with only the minimum-necessary argument. The expertise is used to filter the information and so to remove inessential noise. The manager as expert provides the answers to problems, not an exposition of past and present knowledge. You use your knowledge to focus upon the important points.

When you approach any document, follow this simple procedure:

1) Establish the AIM
2) Consider the READER
3) Devise the STRUCTURE
4) DRAFT the text
5) EDIT and REVISE

That is it. For the rest of this chapter, we will expand upon these points and explain some techniques to make the document effective and efficient – but these five stages (all of them) are what you need to remember.

> *To Practise 5.1:* It is worth actually writing a document as you go through this chapter. Choose something which needs to be done, and which is fairly short (so that you can concentrate on the process of writing).

5.2 Initial Planning

Aim

You start with your *aim*. Every document must have a single aim – a specific, *specified* reason for being written. If you cannot think of one, do something useful instead. If you cannot decide what the document should achieve, it will achieve nothing.

This emphasis upon a single aim is an exaggeration, but only a slight one. The majority of documents you produce will be read only once and quickly. Thus if you are to communicate anything that is remembered, you must focus very strongly upon that point. Typically, you will need to support what you say with argument, facts, conjectures. But essentially you get to make effectively only one point per document.

> *To Practise 5.2:* What is the aim of your document? Need it be written? Have you checked?

The Reader

Once you have established your aim, you must then decide what information is necessary in achieving that aim. The reader wants to find the outcome of your thoughts; apply your expertise to the available information, pick out the very few facts which are relevant, and state them precisely and concisely.

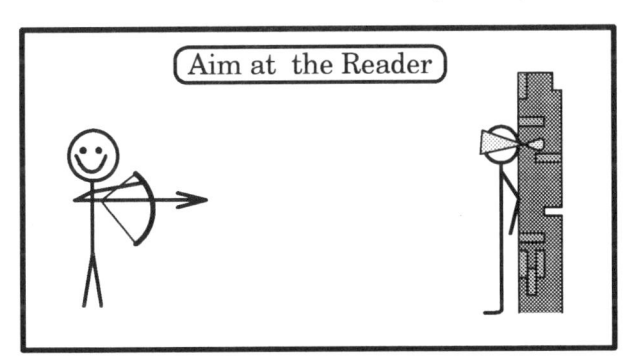

Aim at the Reader

A document tells somebody something. As the writer, you have to decide what to tell and how best to tell it to the particular audience; you must consider the reader. There are three considerations:

- what they already know affects what you can leave out.
- what they need to know determines what you include.
- what they want to know suggests the emphasis of your writing.

If the reader lacks background information, then the writer must supply it; conversely, if the reader already knows a great deal, the writer should not repeat this except to recall the information in the reader's mind. Thus, in deciding which facts are relevant, the wise manager must consider 'relevance' in terms of the reader.

In constructing the order and the emphasis of the document, the writer must consider what the reader wants to achieve. This then becomes the guide in determining the emphasis and opening – so that the reader's concentration is won quickly. For instance, in a product proposal, marketing will want to see the product's differentiation and niche in the market place; finance will be interested in projected development costs, profit margins and risk analysis; and R&D will want the technical details of the design. To be most effective, you may need to produce three different reports for the three different audiences.

> *To Practise 5.3: Write down* (in your notebook) who is the victim. Thinking specifically about that person, sketch the corresponding knowledge for the three considerations above.

Structure
Writing is very powerful – and for this reason, you can exploit it. The power comes from its potential as an efficient and effective means of communication: the power is derived from order and clarity. Structure is used to display that order and clarity, and to present the information so that it is more accessible to the reader.

It all comes down to the problem of the short attention span. You have to provide the information in small manageable chunks, and to use the structure of the document to maintain the context. This process is known as hierarchical decomposition (a good example of unnecessary jargon – see later). Basically, you take the information you need to convey and you split it up to help the reader to put it all back together again. The following diagram illustrates how an aim might be decomposed in this way.

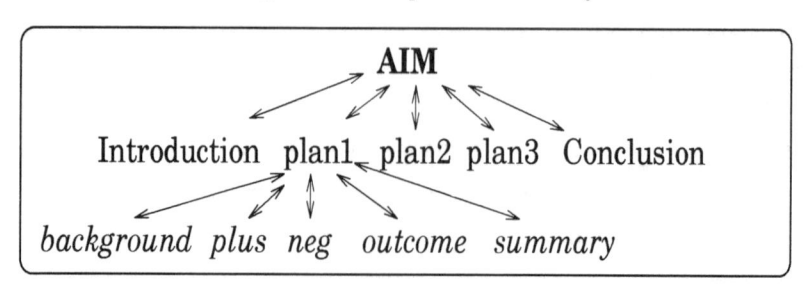

```
                           AIM
              ╱      ╱      ↑      ╲
        Introduction  plan1  plan2  plan3  Conclusion
              ╱      ↑      ╲
    background  plus  neg  outcome  summary
```

While still considering the aim and the reader, the document is broken down into distinct sections which can be written (and *read*) separately. These sections are then each further decomposed into subsections (and sub-subsections) until you arrive at simple, small units of information – which are expressed as a paragraph.

Every paragraph in your document should justify itself; it should serve a purpose, or be removed. A paragraph should convey a single idea. There should be a statement of that key idea and (possibly) some of the following:

- a development of the idea
- an explanation or analogy
- an illustration
- support with evidence
- contextual links to reinforce the structure

To Practise 5.4: Break your aim down into the first layer of sections, and *write* these in your notebook.

As managers, though, you are allowed to avoid words entirely in places; diagrams are often much better than written text. Whole reports can be written with them almost exclusively and you should always consider using one in preference to words. Not only do diagrams convey some information more effectively, but often they assist in the analysis and interpretation of the data. For instance, a pie chart gives a quicker comparison than a list of numbers; a simple bar chart is far more intelligible than the numbers it represents. The only problem with diagrams is that the writer often places less effort in their design than their information-content merits – and so some is lost or obscure. They must be given due care: add *informative* labels and titles, highlight any key entries, remove unnecessary information.

To Practise 5.5: Devise a diagram to illustrate/illuminate one aspect of your document.

5.3 Draft, Revise and Edit

When you have decided what to say, to whom you are saying it, and how to structure it, say it – and then check it for clarity and effectiveness. The time spent doing this will be far less than the time wasted by other people struggling to read your document's first draft.

The key point is that writing is about conveying information – *conveying*; that means it has to get there. Your writing must be right for the reader, or it will be lost on its journey. You must focus upon enabling the reader's access to the information. The following are a few ideas to consider when you wield the red pen over a newly created opus.

Layout
Layout should be used to make the structure plain, and so more effective: it acts as a guide to the reader. The main difference between written and verbal communication is that the reader can choose and re-read the various sections, whereas the listener receives information in the sequence determined by the speaker. Thus your various sections should each have informative titles so that the reader can understand the structure and choose quickly what to read.

Suppose you have three main points to make. Do not hide them within simple text – make them obvious. Make it so that the reader's eye jumps straight to them on the page. For instance, the key to effective layout is to use:

- informative titles
- white space
- ☞ variety

Another way to make a point obvious is to *use a different type face*.

Style
People in business do not have the time to marvel at your florid turn of phrase or alluring alliteration. They want to know what the document is about and (possibly) what it says; there is no real interest in style, *except* for ease of access.

In some articles a summary can be obtained by reading the first sentence of each paragraph. The remainder of each paragraph is simply an expansion upon, or explanation of, the initial sentence. In other writing, the topic is given first in a summary form, and then successively repeated with greater detail each time. This is the pyramid structure favoured by newspapers.

A really short and simple document is likely to be read. This has led to the 'memo culture' in which every communication is condensed to one side of A4. Longer documents need to justify themselves to their readers' attention.

A variation on this is the practice of prefacing any long document with an *executive summary* which allows the 'executive' to obtain the main message of your document in a short space of time (equivalent to reading a memo). Such a section is useful because many people are flattered by being treated as executives and will respond by acting professionally (i.e. by actually reading it). An alternative observation is that if the executive is only going to read the first page, then save trees and keep the document to that size in the first place.

The Beginning

Let us imagine the reader. Let us call her Ms X.

Ms X has a lot to do today. She has to prepare for a meeting tomorrow with the regional VP, to make a call to the German design office, and to dictate several letters concerning safety regulations. This month's process-data has failed to reach her. She is busy and distracted. You have possibly twenty seconds for your document to justify itself to her. If by then it has not explained itself and convinced her that she needs to read it – Ms X will tackle something else. If Ms X is a good manager, she will insist on a rewrite; if not, the document may never be read.

Thus, the beginning of your document is crucial. It must be obvious to the reader *at once* what the document is about, and why it should be read. You need to catch the reader's attention but with greater subtlety than this chapter; few management reports can begin with the word *sex*. Unlike a novel, the management document must not contain 'teasing elevatio·.c of suspense'. Take your 'aim', and either state it or achieve it by the end of the first paragraph. For instance, if you have been evaluating a new software package for possible purchase then your reports might begin: 'Having evaluated the McBlair Design Suite, I recommend that ...'.

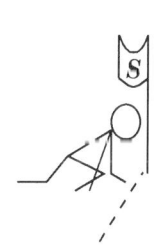

The beginning and end receive the greatest attention

The End

The last section of the document is so often a 'summary and conclusions' that people who read a lot of reports will habitually read the introduction and then cut straight to the last section. If you do not do this yourself, try it; it can save lots of time.

Since this is the case, what does common sense tell you about the ending?

The end is your last chance to restate the conclusive evidence which leads the reader to the evident conclusion you wish to be remembered. Write it with care, and certainly not in the last-minute rush to get the (blo%#*) document finished. If anything gets a rewrite, it should be the beginning-and-end.

Punctuation

Punctuation is used to clarify meaning and to highlight structure. It can also remove ambiguity: a cross section of customers can be rendered less frightening by adding a simple hyphen (a cross-section of customers).

Managers tend not to punctuate – which deprives us of this simple tool. Despite what some remember from school, punctuation has simple rules which lead to elegance and easy interpretation. American and British punctuation are subtly different, but the premise is the same: punctuation aids the reader. Since this is your aim at the moment, try to find a good dictionary (of the chosen variant of English) and read the summary of punctuation which will be lurking in the appendices. Next, apply this new-found wealth to analysing the punctuation in a quality magazine (e.g. *The Economist*) and develop your own style.

For now, let us look at two uses of two punctuation marks. If you do not habitually use these already, add them to your repertoire by deliberately looking for opportunities in your next piece of writing.

The two most common uses of *the Colon* are:

1) to introduce a list which explains, or provides the information promised in, the previous clause:

> *A manager needs two planning tools: prescience and prayer.*

2) to separate main clauses where the second explains or exemplifies the first:

> *Life is like a sewer: what you get out of it, depends on what you put in.*

The two most common uses of *the Semicolon* are:

1) to unite sentences that are closely associated, complementary or parallel:

Writing is a skill; one must practise to improve a skill.

Managers manage; accountants account for the cost.

2) to act as a stronger comma, either for emphasis or to establish a hierarchy:

The report was a masterpiece; of deception and false promises.

The teams were Tom, Martha and Harry; and Mandy, Dick and Mary.

Spelling

For some, spelling is a constant problem. In the last analysis, incorrect speling distracts the reader and detracts from the authority of the author. Computer spell-checking programs provide great assistance, especially when supported by a good dictionary. Chronic spellers should always maintain a (preferably alphabetical) list of corrected errors, and try to learn new rules (and exceptions!). For instance, (in British English) advice-advise, device-devise, licence-license, practice-practise each follow the same pattern: the –ce is a noun, the –se is a verb; American English is generally more relaxed about the whole affair.

Simple Errors

For important documents, there is nothing better than a good, old-fashioned proof-read, especially if undertaken by someone else. As an example, the following comes from a national advertising campaign/quiz run by a famous maker of Champagne:

Question 3: Which Country has one the Triple Crown the most times?

Won understands the error but is ill impressed by that company's concern for quality.

Sentence Length

Avoid long sentences. We tend to associate 'unit of information' with 'a sentence'. Consequently when reading, we process the information when we reach the full stop. If the sentence is too long, we lose the information either because of our limited attention span or because the information was poorly decomposed to start with and might, perhaps, have been broken up into smaller, or possibly better punctuated, sentences which would better have kept the attention of the reader and, by doing so, have reinforced the original message with greater clarity and simplicity.

Word Length
It is inappropriate to utilize verbose and bombastic terminology when a suitable alternative would be: to keep it simple. Often the long, complex word will not be understood. Further, if the reader is distracted by the word itself, then less attention is paid to the meaning or to the information you wish to convey.

A Little Difference
There are no dull subjects. There are only dull writers.
(H L Mencken)

We remember the surprising, not the mundane. If your document is to be effective, it (and your main point) should be made memorable. To achieve this is the challenge. As with formal presentations (chapter 2), you should construct a *hook* upon which the reader will fix and which is associated with your main message. For instance,

> this need not be dramatic, merely different

and a simple change of layout may suffice. Alternatively, you could introduce a quirky turn of phrase or something outwith the established pattern of the document since the jingle of change is as good as a rest.

A simple approach is to construct a phrase to encapsulate your message, and let it repeat itself once or twice in the text, possibly with variations, since through that repetition we remember the sound *and* the message.

Jargon
I believe that a digital human-computer-interface data-entry mechanism should be called a keyboard; I don't know why, but I do.

Wordiness
When one is trying hard to write an impressive document, it is easy to slip into grandiose formulae: words and phrases which sound significant but which convey little but noise.

You must exterminate. So: 'for the reason that' becomes 'because'; 'with regards to' becomes 'about'; 'in view of the fact that' becomes 'since'; 'within a comparatively short period of time' becomes 'soon'.

Often you can make a sentence *sound* more like spoken English simply by changing the word order and adjusting the verb. So: 'if the department experiences any difficulties in the near future regarding attendance of meetings' becomes 'if staff cannot attend any of the next few meetings'. As a final check, read out your document aloud; if it sounds odd, change it.

> *To Practise 5.6:* Now you must write your document – twice. First, write a short document (about 50 words) which says it all. Second, write a full length version (500-2000 words) with careful attention to all the above points. Do a quick first draft following the structure already decided in a previous exercise, and then revise and edit.

5.4 Getting Started

Composing a new document can be difficult. The idea of starting with a main theme and breaking this down into nicely ordered sections and subsections all depends upon you having nicely ordered mind – and a lot of people do not. This is not a slur on their intelligence, but rather a recognition that some creative imaginations work faster than the logical mind can order the thoughts.

For such people, the order of the hierarchical decomposition can be replaced with the anarchy of a *spider chart* (as shown on the next page). A spider chart is an initially blank piece of paper upon which you write your ideas as fast as they emerge. A safe place to start is at the centre of the page with the main *aim* of the document – and then start scribbling ideas all over. The only real proviso is that each new idea should be written next to any related ideas which are already on the chart. When the ideas stop flowing, draw rings around groups of ideas, number them in the order you might present them, and review your artistry.

> *To Practise 5.7:* Spider charts can also be used in group discussions as a variant of brainstorming. Consider what difference (if any) this grouping of ideas might have on the 'flow' of a brainstorming session.

Once you have determined the structure, either by hierarchical decomposition or by trained spiders, you can further plan the document by considering its length. For any work-related document, there will be considerable precedent as to how long it is expected to be. Your aim should be a document of about 80% this size since you will be writing in a *clear, concise* style. With the size of the total document decided, consider the relative importance of the different sections and assign a target length to each. In this way, you have broken down the task of the large document into a set of smaller tasks which can then be written independently. For many people, these will seem less daunting. With a little practice, you will soon get the hang of writing to a fixed length and this can actually help since it often determines whether individual ideas are excluded or expanded to make the section length correspond to its importance.

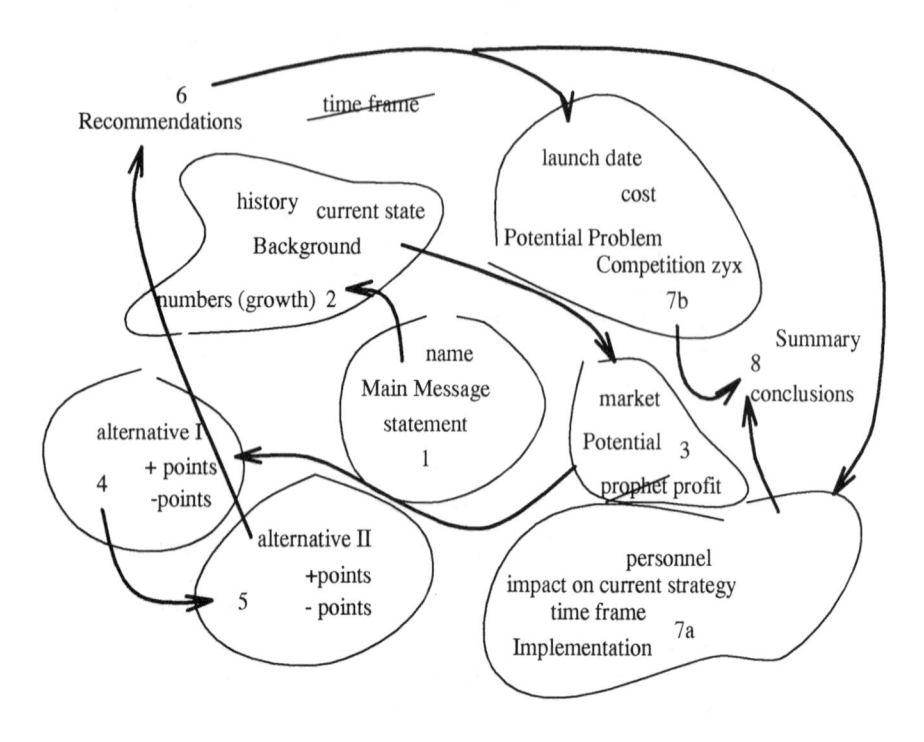

```
          6                time frame
     Recommendations
                                        launch date
                                                        cost
              history   current state
                                        Potential Problem
                 Background                     Competition zyx
        numbers (growth) 2                              7b
                                                                    Summary
                              name                                8
                          Main Message       market          conclusions
       alternative I         statement     Potential  3
           + points              1
        4                                  prophet profit
           -points
                     alternative II
                                             personnel
                        +points         impact on current strategy
                    5    - points             time frame
                                            Implementation  7a
```

5.5 A Small Assignment

Writing is a complex tool. You need to train yourself in its use or a large proportion of your activity will be grossly inefficient. You should reflect upon your writing lest it reflect badly upon you.

> *To Practise 5.8:* Consider the following text (written by a student). Rewrite it so that the information is immediately accessible to the reader.

****

There are two main points that I have learn't from this project about design practise. The first is the importance in thinking about what you are doing and taking time to plan through what you will do rather than jumping straight into a problem. I also learn't the importance of doing a through investigation before you enter the design stage, by when it may be too late to correct your design. I have also learn't the advantages in testing as you go along rather than at the end. Furthermore the importance in trying to keep good notes and records rather than scribbling down an idea with no explanation so that the next time you look at it you can't work out whats going on.

****

Of course, nothing you write would be that bad. Nothing you put on paper would be anything less than clear/accessible. So to convince yourself of the need for this practice of Revise-and-Edit, take the last three documents which landed on your desk and answer the following:

1) What was the document trying to tell you? (in one sentence)
2) Rewrite paragraphs two-to-four in a clearer, more succinct manner.
3) Is the conclusion clearly stated? (re-state it if not)
4) Do you know exactly what you were meant to do once you had read the document (i.e. why was it sent to you in the first place)?
5) Could the message have been relayed more efficiently?

And when you have thus exercised your critical judgement, apply it in the same manner to the last document *you* produced.

Returning to the poor paragraph above, I offer the following comments. There are two levels of error. The first is dealt with simply by using a red pen and attacking the typos, spelling, punctuation and a few of the links between the sentences. The second level requires a good look at the structure and aim of the whole piece, and at how this can be made plain to the reader. If you have not yet done the exercise, pause and do it now. A possible reworking might look as follows:

****

There are four main points-of-practice which emerged during this project:

- take time to think and plan before jumping in
- investigate the design thoroughly before implementing it (when it is too late for corrections)
- test as you go along rather than at the end
- keep good notes rather than scribbles (which will tell you nothing later)

****

This 'fair' solution uses (mostly) the original words and ideas, but with the structure reflected in the layout. Notice that the 'good' ideas are all lined up on the left hand side so that the reader can just pick them off one by one. The point is that the student did have four(!) good points – but without a little revision, they did not impress themselves quickly upon the reader.

The above example demanded a complete rewrite – mostly your documents merely need a bit of polishing. If your documents are produced on a word-processor, then you have no excuse. Get a first draft printed out, double-spaced, and sit quietly in the corner (with coffee, doughnuts and red pen) to revise and edit carefully. At one level, look particularly for the flow of ideas between paragraphs and the merits of the overall structure; at the lower level, check for spelling and punctuation. Each word might be replaced with a simpler one; each phrase may allow a better idiom; each concept may be better expressed and/or illustrated; if a word offends thee, pluck it out. If you do this with each document, *you learn* to write better and so will recoup the time in faster composition and revision in the future. This is effective management of your own time and skills development.

Improving writing skills is possible for any manager no matter how good (or bad) you are already. As with all such skills, it is simply a case of deliberate effort. As a start, there are many reference books where points of style and correct usage are explained in detail – your team should have access to these books, and you should be seen to use them yourself. Using the company's money (which is always fun) buy two or three such guides and put them in the office where they can be seen. If in doubt, ask a secretary to purchase them for you; he/she is likely to recognize what will be most helpful.

As an exercise, you should now write a couple of short pieces purely to focus upon the process of writing. The task is to rewrite this chapter. The first document is to be less than one-side of A4 (typed, single spaced): a maximum of 500 words; the second document is five times that size (2000-2500 words) and should be aimed at an audience composed purely of people like Arnold (whose documents you have to read). These compositions are not simply condensed versions of this chapter. You have to extract the information and rewrite it in your own style and words within the specified limits; you will have to be selective in deciding what to include and what to exclude.

As a practical step forward, use this chapter and any other reference material to devise a 'checklist' for revising and editing first drafts. Write it as a step-by-step procedure for examining documents with an emphasis on ease of use rather than completeness (i.e. do not try to copy out every rule of grammar). Under no circumstances should you call it a documentation standard, or no one will ever read it. Instead, call it something like a help-list or a fast-checker. Either circulate this around your team asking for comments and suggestions, or simply leave copies lying around your desk (or next to the reference books) where they will be noticed.

To play *Watch the Manager* you simply have to read each document that finishes on your desk with a pencil in your hand. When the writing goes wrong, put a line through the offending passage; when something is done particularly well, circle it with a tick in the margin. If the document comes from your team, always praise the best aspect; occasionally, you should suggest improvements.

If you want one message to take from this chapter, take this: a manager's writing should be clear, complete and concise. If your document satisfies these three criteria, then it deserves to be read.

Summary of Writing

Consider 'why?'   (Aim the document)
Write (right) for the Reader
Keep it
   - Short and Simple
   - Complete but Concise
Use Diagrams
Use Structure   (in headings and layout)

what the READER		
already knows	needs to know	wants to know
determines		
what to exclude	what to include	how to start

STRUCTURE . . . .

   is used to order the information so that
   it is accessible to the reader

REVISE AND EDIT

   double-spaced copy and a good red pen

Time spent on managing your writing
reduces time spent on writing

Chapter: 6
The Gentle Art of Delegation

I delegate myne auctorite
(Jehan Palsgrave, 1530)

Everyone knows about delegation. Most managers heard about it in the cradle as mother talked earnestly to the baby-sitter: 'just make yourself at home ... this is what to do if ... if there is any trouble call me at ...'. People have been writing about it for nearly half a millennium; yet few actually understand it.

Delegation underpins a style of management which allows your staff to use and develop their skills and knowledge to the full potential. Without delegation, you lose their full value. As the quotation above suggests, delegation is primarily about entrusting your authority to others. This means that they can act and initiate independently; and that they assume responsibility *with you* for certain tasks. If something goes wrong, you remain responsible since you are the manager – the trick is to delegate in such a way that things get done without going (badly) wrong.

One of the main phobias about delegation is that by giving authority to others, a manager loses control. This need not be the case. If you train your team to apply the same criteria as you would yourself (by example and full explanations) then they will be exercising your control on your behalf. And since they will witness many more situations over which control may be exercised (you can only be in one place at a time) then that control is exercised more diversely and more rapidly than you could exercise it alone. Thus despite what many think, delegation allows you to *increase* your control over events.

6.1 Planning to Delegate

The objective

The objective of delegation is to get the job done by someone else. Not just the simple tasks of reading instructions and turning a lever, but also the decision-making and changes which depend upon new information. With delegation, your staff have the authority to react to situations without referring back to you.

If you tell the janitor to empty the bins on Tuesdays and Fridays, the bins will be emptied on Tuesdays and Fridays. If the bins overflow on Wednesday, they will be emptied on Friday. If instead you said to empty the bins as often as necessary, the janitor would decide how often and adapt to special circumstances. You might suggest a regular schedule (teach the janitor a little time management), but by leaving the decision up to the janitor you will apply his/her local knowledge to the problem. Consider this frankly. Do you want to be an expert on bin emptying? Can you construct an instruction to cover all possible contingencies? If not, delegate to someone who gets paid for it.

To enable others to do the job for you, you must ensure that:

- they know what you want
- they have the authority to achieve it
- they know how to do it.

These all depend upon communicating clearly the nature of the task, the extent of their discretion, and the sources of relevant information and knowledge.

Choosing what to delegate

There is always the question of what to delegate and what to do yourself, and you must take a long-term view on this: you want to delegate as much as possible to develop your staff to be as good as you are now.

The starting point is to consider the activities you used to do before you were promoted. You used to do them when you were more junior, so someone junior can do them now. Tasks in which you have experience are the easiest for you to explain to others and so to train them to take over. You thus use your experience to ensure that the task is done well, rather than actually perform the task yourself. In this way you gain time for your other duties and someone else becomes as good as you once were, thus increasing the strength of the group.

Tasks in which your staff have more experience must be delegated to them. This does not mean that you relinquish responsibility because they are expert, but it does mean that the default decision should be theirs. To be a good manager though, you should ensure that they spend some time in explaining these decisions to you so that you learn their criteria.

Taking decisions is a normal managerial function – these too should be delegated, especially if they are important to the staff. In practice, you will need to establish the scope of the decision so that you can live with the outcome, but this will only take you a little time while the delegation of the remainder of the task will save you much more.

To maintain motivation, you should delegate the more mundane tasks as evenly as possible; and sprinkle the more exciting ones as widely. In general, but especially with the boring tasks, you should be careful to allocate not only the performance of the task but also its ownership. Task delegation, rather than task assignment, enables innovation. The point you need to get across is that the task may be changed, developed, or upgraded, if necessary or desirable. So someone who collates the monthly figures should not feel obliged to blindly type them in every first Monday, but should be empowered to introduce a more effective reporting format, to use computer software to enhance the data processing, to suggest and implement changes to the task itself.

> *To Practise 6.1:* Choose something to delegate from the tasks you currently perform. *Write it* in your notebook.

Staggered development
To understand delegation, you really have to think about people. Delegation cannot be viewed as an abstract technique, it depends upon individuals and individual needs. Let us take a lowly member of staff who has little or no knowledge about the job which needs to be done (remember Arnold?).

Do you say: 'Arnold, I want a draft proposal for the new Industry Link grant on my desk by Friday'?

No! Do you say: 'Arnold, Anabel used to do the grant applications for me. Spend about an hour with her going over how she did them and try compiling one for the new Industry Link grant. She will help you for this one, but do come to me if she is busy. I want a draft by Friday so that we can go over it together'?

Much better. The key is to delegate gradually. If you present someone with a task which is daunting, one with which he/she does not feel able to cope, then the task will not be done and he/she will be severely demotivated. Instead you should build up gradually; first a small task leading to a little development, then another small task which builds upon the first; when that is achieved, add another stage; and so on. This is the difference between asking people to scale a sheer wall and providing them with a staircase: by staggering the delegation you allow them to climb with confidence. Each task delegated should have enough complexity to stretch that member of staff – but only a little and there should always be support available.

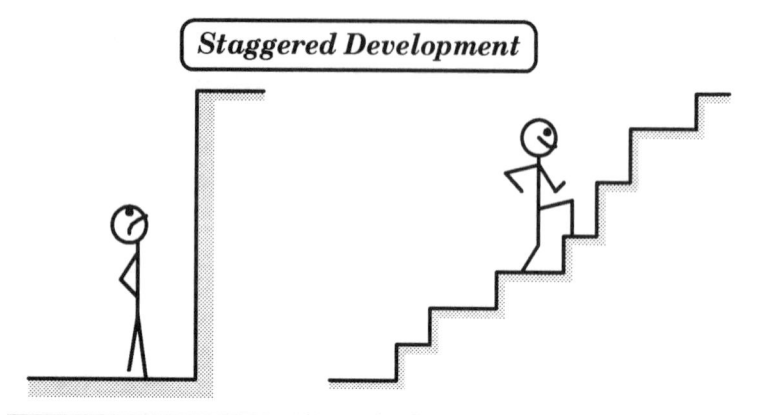

Staggered Development

To Practise 6.2: Consider whether your chosen task is too large a leap for Arnold. If so, devise a sequence of steps by which Arnold can build up to undertaking that task gradually. *Write these down* and decide for each what must happen before Arnold is ready to progress to the next.

Information

Delegation can only operate successfully if the decision-makers (your staff) have full and rapid access to the relevant information. This means that you must establish a system to enable the flow of information. This must at least include regular exchanges amongst your staff so that each is aware of what the others are doing. It should also include briefings by you on the information which you have received in your role as manager; since if you need to know this information to do your job, your staff will need to know it also if they are to do your (delegated) job for you.

One of the main claims being made for computerized information distribution is that it facilitates the rapid dissemination of information. Some protagonists even suggest that such systems will instigate changes in managerial power-sharing rather than merely supporting such changes; that the *enknowledged* workforce will rise up, assume control and innovate spontaneously. You may not believe this vision, but you should understand the premise. If you restrict access to information, then only you are able to make decisions which rely upon that information; once that access is opened to others, they too can make decisions – and challenge yours. The manager who fears this challenge will never delegate effectively; the manager who recognizes that the staff may have additional experience and knowledge (and so may enhance the decision-making process) will welcome their input; delegation ensures that the staff will practise decision-making and will know that their views are welcome.

> *To Practise 6.3:* Consider the task you are delegating. What information is necessary to that task? Can Arnold acquire it himself? If it normally comes to you, could it be passed directly to him? Could someone else act as a coach to Arnold as he becomes familiar with the task?

6.2 Support and Monitoring

When a task is delegated it assumes a life of its own. It can grow and multiply, change its shape, devour time and confidence, and generally be a bit of a pest. For the person given that task, it can seem very frightening. The problem is that since you have few fears about these tasks yourself, you forget that others might and so a delegated task is often forgotten – until the beast has triplets which run riot through your schedules.

Since delegation is about handing over authority, you cannot dictate precisely what is delegated nor how it is managed. To *control* the delegation, you need to establish at the beginning:

- the task itself
- the reporting schedule
- the sources of information
- the availability of support
- the criteria for success

These you must *negotiate* with your staff. Only by obtaining both their input and their agreement can you hope to arrive at a workable procedure. There are two distinct outcomes from your interaction with the Arnold:

- he gains your assistance
- you monitor progress so that you can intervene (gently but quickly) if something goes wrong.

Arnold needs to feel confident. He needs to believe that he will actually be able to achieve the task which has been given to him. This means that either he must have sufficient knowledge, or he must know where to get it or where to get help. So, you must *enable access to the necessary knowledge*. If you hold that knowledge, make sure that Arnold feels able to come to you; if someone else holds the knowledge, make sure that they are prepared for Arnold to come to them. Only if Arnold is sure that support is available will he feel confident enough to undertake a new responsibility.

You need to feel confident in Arnold: this means keeping an eye on him. It would be fatal to cast Arnold adrift and expect him to make it to the shore; keep an eye on him, and a lifebelt handy. It is also a mistake to keep wandering up to Arnold at odd moments and asking for progress reports: he will soon feel persecuted. Instead you must agree beforehand how often and when you actually need information and *decide the reporting schedule at the outset*. Arnold will then anticipate these encounters and even feel encouraged by your continuing support; you will be able to check upon progress and even spur it on a little.

Each distinct pairing of people and tasks will require a different level of monitoring and support. In deciding this level, you must consider not only the general capabilities of the person, but also any specific knowledge he/she might have about the particular task. Furthermore, the necessary level of support will change as the task progresses since the person's knowledge and confidence will also be changing.

Plan   Mon - i - tor   Re - view

Do not stint in your monitoring on the grounds that Arnold needs space to make mistakes – if you are not watching carefully the mistakes can grow large enough to damage his confidence. If you catch mistakes in time, they can be remedied by a simple suggestion (which Arnold 'might like to consider') rather than by you resuming control.

While you must always offer support, there is a danger in allowing your team 'open access' to your help in that you can become too involved with the task you had hoped to delegate. One successful strategy to avoid this is to formalize the manner in which these conversations take place. One formalism is to allow only fixed, regular encounters (except for emergencies) so that Arnold has to think about issues and questions before raising them; you might even insist that he draws up an agenda. A second formalism is to refuse to make a decision unless Arnold has provided you with a clear statement of alternatives, pros and cons, and *his recommendation*.

Format for Decision-Making

Statement of Problem

Solution ONE
  Advantages
  Disadvantages

Solution TWO
  Advantages
  Disadvantages

Solution THREE
  +ve
  -ve

Solution ETC
  +ve
  -ve

Recommendation

This is my favourite. It allows Arnold to rehearse the full authority of decision making while still being secure in the knowledge that you will be there to check the outcome. Further, the insistence upon evaluation of alternatives promotes good decision-making practices. If Arnold is right, then Arnold's confidence increases – if you disagree with Arnold, he learns something new (provided you explain your criteria) and so his knowledge increases. Whichever way, he benefits; and the analysis is provided for you.

Similarly, whenever you talk to Arnold about the project, you should avoid taking charge: do your own job, not his. The whole idea is for Arnold to learn to take over and thus he must be encouraged to do so. Of course, with you there to check his decisions, Arnold will feel freer to take more control. If Arnold is wrong – tell him, and explain very carefully why. If Arnold is nearly right – congratulate him, and suggest possible modifications; but, of course, leave Arnold to decide. Finally, unless your solution has *significant* merits over Arnold's, take his; it costs you little, yet rewards him much.

The manner of your interaction can also depend upon the person. Some people will respond well to the informal chat over coffee, some would feel happier with a formal, regular report covering the agreed issues. You will have to decide upon how, and how often, *habitually* to check upon progress and problems.

> *To Practise 6.4:* Choose a reporting strategy for the first stage of the planned delegation. Consider how to explain it *clearly and completely* to Arnold, and how to monitor progress.

6.3 Outcomes and Failure

Experience is the name everyone gives to their mistakes
(Oscar Wilde)

Let us consider your undoubtedly high standards. When you delegate a job, it does not have to be done as well as you could do it (given time), but only as well as necessary – never judge the outcome by what you expect you would do (it is difficult to be objective about that) but rather by fitness for purpose. When you delegate a task, agree then upon the criteria and standards by which the outcome will be judged.

You must enable failure. With appropriate monitoring, you should be able to catch mistakes before they are catastrophic; if not, then the failure is yours. You are the manager, you decided that Arnold could cope, you gave him enough rope to hang himself, you are at fault. Now that that is cleared up, let us return to Arnold. Suppose Arnold gets something wrong; what do you want to happen?

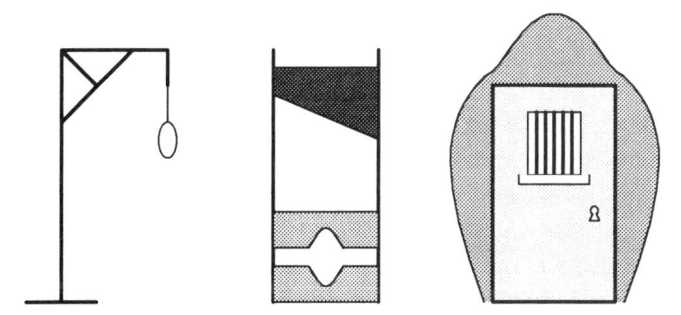

Firstly, you want it fixed. Since Arnold made the mistake, it is likely that he will need some input to develop a solution; so Arnold must feel safe in approaching you with the problem. Thus you must deal primarily with the solution rather than chastising Arnold (look forward, not backwards). The most desirable outcome is that Arnold provides the solution himself.

Once that is dealt with, you can analyse the cause. Do not fudge the issue; if Arnold did something wrong say so, but only in very specific terms. Avoid general attacks on his childhood: 'were you born this stupid?', and look to the actual event or circumstance which led to the error: 'did you take account of X in your decision?'.

Your objectives are to ensure that Arnold:

- understands the problem
- feels confident enough to resume
- implements some procedure to prevent recurrence.

The safest ethos to cultivate is one where Arnold actually looks for and anticipates mistakes. If you wish to promote such behaviour, you should always praise Arnold for his prompt and wise action in spotting and dealing with the errors rather that castigate him for causing them. Here the emphasis is placed upon checking/testing/monitoring. Thus you never criticize Arnold for finding an error, only for not having safeguards in place.

> *To Practise 6.5:* For your chosen task, think carefully what might go wrong with Arnold in charge for the first time. There must be at least three ways this can happen; try brainstorming on the theme of 'catastrophe'. Do not lose heart, but establish mechanisms to provide early warning of each of the identified dangers and explain them to Arnold.

6.4 Making Time

Now is the time to think seriously about what you do. As a manager you have responsibility for your team and its projects – to fulfil that responsibility properly takes a lot of time and thought – delegation is a means for creating that time.

From your analysis of your own work (in chapter 4), list the different jobs which you currently do (how you spend your time).

Against each and every one of these, write the name of one of your team who is suited one day to take over this job from you. This includes even the big jobs since the No.13 bus may strike you at any time and someone would have to take over. Make sure that everyone in your team appears on the list (even Arnold) and that no one appears too often.

For each job-person pair, devise a plan of *staggered development* by which that person could be gradually trained through increased responsibility to take that job on permanently.

You must now consider that your own manager may be reading this book and doing exactly the same exercise. If this is so, you will very soon be receiving even more tasks with further responsibility. Thus you should start now to make time in your busy schedule. You should start the process of delegating your current workload so that you can take on the work which your manager is planning to give to you (how else will you progress?).

So, devise a plan of staggered development to delegate one of your jobs to each person in your team starting this week.

Summary of Delegation

Clear specification of Task
    Actual authority to get the job done
        Access to necessary knowledge

DELEGATION ENHANCES YOUR CONTROL

> Delegate
> - what you are good at
> - what they are good at
> - what affects them
> - as much as possible

Encourage decision-making by insisting on 'recommendations'

> Establish clearly
> - task
> - reporting schedule
> - information
> - support
> - criteria for success

Match manner/complexity of delegation
to both the person and the task

Vary this over time as the situation changes

Enable failure - but insist on recovery

Chapter: 7
To Capture Quality

Come, give us a taste of your quality
(Hamlet II ii – William Shakespeare)

Quality has become the philosophers' stone of management practice with consultants and gurus vying to charm lead-laden corporations into gold-winning champions. Stories abound of base companies with morose workers and mounting debts being transformed into happy teams and healthy profits; never a day goes by without a significant improvement, a pounds-saving suggestion or a quantum leap in efficiency. There are, however, several problems with the popular view of '*Quality*' which deserve a little consideration.

As it is commonly portrayed, quality is something which can only be achieved through an extensive programme which is company-wide and led by senior management. The advocates of this view of quality are addressing corporate leaders who wish to transform the whole company; quality is sold to them as a panacea for all their woes. This view gives the little guy very little encouragement to go it alone – which is reasonable if you are engineering the salvation of the company. However, quality can (and should) be readily applied by any manager with his/her own team.

Another problem with many quality programmes is that they are forced to follow a rigid formula. Again, this stems from the emphasis on a company-wide programme which must be communicated and implemented by all; a standard programme is easier to monitor and explain. Thus, the quality programme (though initially fresh) soon becomes yet another standard procedure, a part of the bureaucracy, and the existence of a mandated structure reduces the degree of flexibility with which individual teams can respond to unique circumstances and changes.

A final flaw in the popular view of quality is that many programmes lay strong emphasis on the creation of specialist teams dedicated to single tasks. The theory here is that the teams are formed by people from several work groups to promote inter-group communication and to tackle problems which span over (and so are ignored by) many different groups. This is, of course, a laudable idea. However, the focus is thus placed upon activity external to any one team, and away from the the ordinary, daily, bread-and-butter activity of the company's workforce.

These criticisms do not invalidate the ideas of quality – they are made simply to suggest that the principles may well be viewed from a fresh angle – and applied at a different level. This chapter attempts to provide a new perspective by re-examining some of the tenets of quality in the context of a small, established team (like yours). Simply, what can you, as a manager, do for your own team through the application of quality?

7.1 What is 'Quality'?

In current management writings 'Quality' has come to refer to a whole gamut of practices which themselves have resulted in beneficial side-effects; as a manager, you will want to take advantage of these benefits also. We will consider four aspects of quality as it has evolved in general management theory and as it might be applied by you to your group.

> *To Practise 7.1:* First of all, consider what you mean when *you* talk of quality.

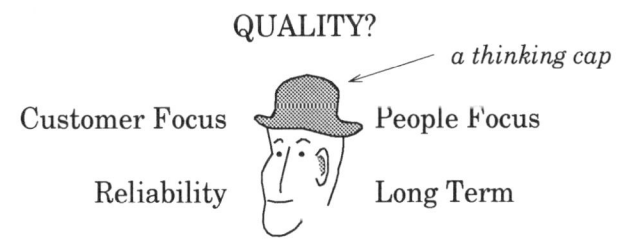

QUALITY?

a thinking cap

Customer Focus   People Focus

Reliability   Long Term

The customer
In simple terms, attaining quality has something to do with satisfying the expectations of *the customer*; the wishes and needs of customers become the focus for every decision. What the customer wants, the company provides. This is not philanthropy, this is basic survival. Through careful education by competitors, the customer has begun to exercise spending power in favour of quality goods and services; and while quality is not the only criterion, it has become an important differentiator.

If one ball-point pen breaks in one month and another ball-point pen lasts for three, then the second ball-point pen is the pen which the customer will buy again and which he/she recommends to others — even if it costs a little more. The makers of the first ball-point pen may have a higher profit margin, but eventually they will have no sales; without quality in the product, a company sacrifices customers, revenue and ultimately its own existence. In practical terms, quality is that something extra which will be perceived by the customer as a valid reason for either paying more or for buying again.

In the case where the product is a service, quality is equated with how well the job is done and especially with whether the customer is made to *feel good* about the whole operation. A quality service may cost a little more to provide, but the cost is recouped in the price customers are prepared to pay and in the increase of business.

Now, apply this in terms of your own team. In most cases, there is no actual money changing hands — most teams in industry do not actually sell anything. What you produce is part of the whole company's product, either directly or as a support service. Your customer is thus found somewhere in the rest of the company, and your 'payment' is the reputation of, and the perceived need for, your team. Thus the model of 'customer satisfaction' in the context of your own small team implies that you should gain recognition within the company: 'that team does good work!'

> *To Practise 7.2:* Identify your team's customers. The simplest place to start is at the interfaces between the team and the rest of company: who do they talk to, who benefits from what they do, who would come running if you all went on holiday? *Write down* at least three.

> *To Practise 7.3:* Harder, consider your own customers. As a manager you are an interface between your team (one set of customers), other managers at your own level (another set), and the gods that rule you all (a third set). For each set, identify *two* functions which you perform — and, for one of the six functions, consider how to perform it in a slightly different manner to make that customer happier.

Reliability
In manufacturing, the clearest manifestation of quality is in a product's *reliability*: that the product works and continues to do so. To prevent problems from arising after the product is shipped, the quality must be checked before-hand – and the best time to check quality is throughout the *whole* design and production cycle. The old method of quality control was to test the completed product and then to rework to remove any problems. Thus, while the original production time was short, the rework time was long. The new approach to quality simply asserts that if testing becomes an integral part of each stage of production, the production time may increase but the rework time will disappear. Further, you will catch and solve many problems which the final 'big-bang' quality-check would miss but which the customer would find on the first day.

To achieve this approach requires an environment where the identification of errors is considered to be 'a good thing', where the only bad *bugs* are the ones which get away. One of the most hallowed doctrines of quality is that of *zero defects*. 'Zero defects' is a focus, it is a glorious objective, it is the assertion that nothing less than perfection will suffice and that no matter how high the quality of a product, it can still be improved. It is a paradox in that it is an aim which is contrary to reason, and, like the paradoxes of many other religions, it holds an inner truth. This is why the advocates of quality often seem a little crazy: they are zealots.

If your team provides more of a service than a product, this idea of reliability still applies. You must simply view what you produce and decide (honestly) how often your team produces work of which you are proud.

> *To Practise 7.4:* Suppose your team's customers were offered real money for each valid/sensible (to be decided by your boss) criticism/suggestion about the product/service your team is providing. *Write down* the aspect of your team's work which would receive the most attention.

People as resource
While quality has its own reward in terms of long-term success, the methods used to achieve this quality have other benefits. In seeking to improve the quality of their products, manufacturers discovered that the people best placed to make substantial contributions are the workforce: *people are the most valuable resource*. It is this shift in perspective from the management to the workforce which is the most significant consequence of the search for quality. From it has arisen a new managerial philosophy aimed at the empowerment of the workforce, decision-making by the front line, and

active worker involvement in the company's advancement. From this new perspective, new organizational structures have evolved, exemplified in 'Quality Circles'.

It is important to examine the consequences of this approach. To apply such a philosophy safely and effectively, the management has to train the workforce. They have to learn how to hold meetings, how to analyse problems, how to take decisions, how to present solutions, how to implement and evaluate change. These traditionally high-level managerial prerogatives are devolved to the whole staff.

Not only does this develop talent, it also stimulates interest. Staff begin to look not only for problems but also for solutions. Simple ideas become simply implemented: the secretary finally gets the filing cabinet moved closer to the desk, the sales meetings follow an agenda, the software division creates a new bulletin board for the sports club. The environment is created where people see problems and fix 'em.

Larger problems have more complex solutions. One outcome of the search for quality in Japan is the system of Just-In-Time flow control. In this system, goods arrive at each stage of the manufacturing process just before they are needed, and are not made until they are needed for the next stage. This reduces storage requirements and the inventory costs of surplus stock. Another outcome has been the increased flexibility of the production line. The time required to change from one product run to the next was identified as a major obstacle in providing the customer with the desired range of products and lot sizes, and so the whole workforce became involved in changing extant practices and even in redesigning the machinery.

This is why quality is so powerful a concept to apply to your own team. It has now acquired a tradition which allows everybody in the team to make their own contribution and to utilize their own special experience and expertise. With this prerogative, whole new practices and solutions to problems will flow from their initiative. No longer will you, the manager, have to think of changes to help the team. Instead you will be having to vet the multitude of proposals which arise from those best placed to innovate. At least that is the theory – as you can see, quality has many zealots.

The long term
However, the most significant shift in perspective which accompanies the introduction of quality is that long-term success is given precedence over short-term gains. Repeat-sales and recommendations become more important than this month's sales figures; staff training and development

remain in place despite immediate scheduling problems; the product's reliability becomes paramount, even over time-to-market. Time is devoted today to saving time in the future and in making products which work first and every time.

Because the focus is moved away from the immediate task, it can fall instead upon the methods of the work itself. Thus the work practices and systems are scrutinized and if these can be improved, time is devoted to this before the project itself. Since the focus is upon the work practices, it is the workers themselves who are in the position to offer the best suggestions. Through them, the manager begins to manage the actual process of work rather than a sequence of disjoint projects.

To achieve this you, as a manager, must communicate to your group the role of Planner: your own focus on the future. The future is important; you have to cater for it in your decision making about their work; the team must know, understand and see that this is a priority.

7.2 Team Quality

While the salvation of an entire corporation may rest primarily with Senior Management, the fate of a team rests with their own manager. As team leader, you have the authority, the power, to define the micro-culture of the work team. It is by the deliberate application of the principles of quality that you can gain for the team the same benefits which quality can provide for a corporation.

Quality

The best ideas for any particular team are likely to come from them – your aim should be to act as a catalyst, through prompts and by example. The following are possible suggestions on how to make the search for quality a rallying focus for the building of your team.

Getting started

There will be no overnight success. To be lasting, quality must become a habit and a habit is accustomed practice. This takes time and training – not necessarily formal training but possibly the sort of reinforcement you might give to any aspect of good practice. To habituate your staff to quality, you must first make it an issue. Here are two suggestions.

The first idea is to become enthusiastic about one aspect at a time, and initially to look for a quick kill. Find a problem and start to talk about it with the whole team; do not delegate it to an individual but make it an issue for everybody. Choose some work-related problem like 'how to get the right information in time' and solicit everybody's views and suggestions – and get the problem solved. Demand urgency against a clear target. There is no need to allocate large amounts of resource or time to this, simply raise the problem and make a fuss. When a solution comes, praise it by rewarding the whole team and ensure that the aspects of increased efficiency, productivity, and calm are highlighted since this will establish the criteria for 'success'. Next, find another problem and repeat.

> *To Practise 7.5:* Consider the issue you selected previously. Decide how to broach it with the *whole* of your team.

The second idea is to hold a regular meeting to discuss quality. Of course meetings can be complete time wasters, so this strategy requires care. The benefits are that regularity will lead to habit, the formality will provide a simple opportunity for the expression of ideas, and the inclusion of the whole group at the meeting will emphasize the collective responsibility. By using the regular meeting, you can establish the 'ground rules' of accepted behaviour and at the same time train the team in effective techniques.

> *To Practise 7.6:* Another way to prepare for either strategy is to canvass for ideas. During next week, make a point of talking to each of your team informally and asking about: ideas for improvement, problems with other groups, any little (long-term) jobs that need doing but never seem to get done. Make a list, choose a strategy.

One problem is that the focus on any one particular issue may quickly lose its impact. The solution is to have frequent shifts in focus so that you maintain the freshness and enthusiasm. A further benefit is that continual shifts in emphasis will train your team to be flexible and provide the opportunity for them to raise new issues. The sooner the team takes over the definition of the 'next problem', the better.

Initial phases

The initial phases are delicate, especially if you are using this to introduce team building. The team will be feeling greater responsibility without extra confidence. Thus you must concentrate on supporting their development. Essentially you will be their trainer in management skills. You could get outside help with this but by undertaking the job yourself, you retain control: you mould the team so that they will reflect your own approach and use your own criteria. Later they will develop themselves, but even then they will understand your thinking and so your decisions.

One trap to avoid is that the team may focus upon the wrong type of problem. You must make it clear that any problem they tackle should be:

- related to their own work or environment
- something which they can change

This precludes gripe sessions about wages and holidays.

As with all group work, the main problem is clarity. You should provide the team with a notice board and flip-charts specifically for quality problems. These can then be left on display as a permanent record of what was agreed, and hopefully as an inspiration.

If you can, steer the group first to some problem to which there is a simple solution with obvious (measurable) benefits. Nothing motivates like a quick, sharp success.

Team building

To succeed, a quality drive must engage the enthusiasm of the entire team; as the manager, you must create the right atmosphere for this to happen. Many aspects of team building can be addressed while quality remains the focus.

You must create the environment where each team member feels totally free to express an idea or concern, and this can only be done if there is no stigma attached to being incorrect. *No idea is wrong – merely non-optimal.* In each suggestion there is at least a thread of gold and someone should point it out and, if possible, build upon it. Any behaviour which seeks laughter at the expense of others must be swiftly reprimanded.

One crude but effective method is to write down agreed ground rules and to display them as a constant reminder for everyone, something like:

- all criticism must be kind and constructive
- *bugs WANTED: dead or alive* (but not for long)
- if it saves time later, do it *NOW*

> *To Practise 7.7:* Dream up a war cry for your team. Write it large and hang it over your desk.

Another method is to constantly talk about the group with the plural pronoun: 'we decided', 'we can do this', 'we'll get back to you'. This is especially effective if it is used in conversation with outsiders (particularly senior management) within ear-shot of the team. Praise and reward the whole team; get the team wider fame by publicizing successes throughout the company.

Most importantly, you must enable failure. If the team is unable to try out ideas without rebuke for errors, then the scope of their solutions will be severely limited. Instead, a failure should be an opportunity to gain knowledge and to praise any safe-guards which were included in the plan.

Mutual coaching

An important aspect of team interaction is the idea of mutual support. If you can instil the idea that all problems are owned by the entire team then each member will be able to seek help and advice when needed from everyone else. One promoter of this is to encourage mutual coaching. If one team member knows techniques and information which would be useful to the rest, then encourage him/her to share them. This will raise the profile, confidence and self-esteem of the instructor at the same time as benefiting the entire group. And if there is one member who might never have anything useful to impart – send him/her to a conference or training session to learn something.

Statistics

One of the central tenets of quality programmes is the idea of monitoring the problem being addressed: *Statistical Quality Control*. Quite simply, if you cannot measure an improvement, it probably is not there. Gathering statistics has several benefits in applying quality:

- it identifies (the extent of) the problem
- it allows progress to be monitored
- it provides an objective criterion for the abandonment of an idea
- it can justify perceived expense in terms of observed savings or improvements
- it motivates staff by providing a display of achievement

and some problems simply disappear when you try to watch them.

The statistics must be gathered in an objective and empirical manner, the outcome should be a simple table or graph regularly updated to indicate progress, and these results *must be displayed* where all the team can watch. For example, if your team provides product support, then you might monitor and graph the number of repeat enquiries or the average response time. If you are in product development, you might monitor the number of bugs discovered before release (i.e. improvement opportunities).

In the long term, it might be possible to automate the gathering of statistics on a wide range of issues such as complaints, bug reports, machine downtime, etc. Eventually these would either provide early warning of unexpected problems, or comparative data for new quality improvement projects. It is vital, however, that they focus upon an agreed problem and not upon an individual's performance, or else all the positive motivation of staff involvement will be lost.

> *To Practise 7.8:* For the problem you identified earlier, decide how to measure it and to whom you might give that job. (If you choose the right person, the problem may be solved without your further action – if so, do that and choose the next problem).

Bugs in perspective
When you have identified a problem it is unwise to treat it at face value. Often the first bug you see is merely a symptom rather than the problem itself and you should delve deeply to establish the root causes. If you use a quick, *ad hoc* fix you are likely to hide the bug rather than kill it, and it will simply crawl around your 'fix' and appear again somewhere else.

Another problem with bugs is that people often believe that they are singular, whereas in reality they normally travel in packs. Suppose you were a chef in a restaurant and just before you sent the salad bowl into the dining room, a cockroach crawled out of the bowl onto the table. If you then managed to decapitate the bug with a handy cleaver would you say: 'Oh rapture! I've killed *the* bug', and then send the salad bowl to the dining table? Of course not. You would go very carefully through all the salad materials looking for other bugs which would undoubtedly be lurking, waiting, wanting to entertain your customers. This should also be your attitude when you start killing bugs in your search for quality. Dealing with one bug is not the end of the search, it is only the beginning.

Specifying projects

Clarity of purpose – this is the key to success. You need a simple, stated objective which everybody understands and which everybody can see achieved.

Any specification to improve quality must contain:

- the aim
- the method
- the statistical display for monitoring the outcome
- the agreed criteria for completion or curtailment

By insisting on this format, you provide the plan-owners with a simple mechanism for peer recognition (through the displayed notice board) and yet enable them to manage their own failure with grace.

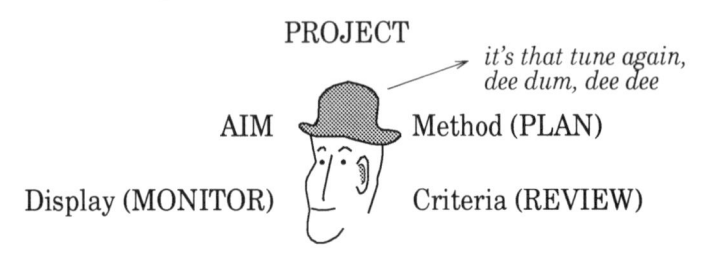

PROJECT

it's that tune again, dee dum, dee dee

AIM   Method (PLAN)

Display (MONITOR)   Criteria (REVIEW)

Check the interfaces

For a small established team, the 'customer' includes any part of the company with which the team interacts. Thus, any themes regarding customer satisfaction can be developed with respect to these so-called *internal customers*. In the end, the effectiveness of your team will be judged by the reports of how well they provide products or services for others.

The interfaces are usually the best place to look for simply solved problems. A simple innovation might be for a member of your team to actually talk to someone from each of these internal customer groups, and to ask about problems. The immediate benefit may be to the customer, but in the long run better communications will lead to fewer misunderstandings and so less rework.

Building Quality

Quality costs less than its lack; look after the pennies and the profits will take care of themselves. To build a quality product, you must do two things:

- 'worry' the work and the procedures
- include features to aid quality checking

As a dog worries a bone, so you (and your team) should worry the practices and systems upon which the work depends. It is a question of attitude: you should allocate time specifically to discussing improvements. If one of the team spots a modification which will have a long-term benefit, then that must be given priority over the immediate schedule. Often the search for quality does not result in extra features in the work; instead the aim should be for simplicity, to eliminate the complex so that problems are avoided. Another aim is to provide mechanisms for the prediction of problems. Thus the 'process' of work becomes explicitly managed (by the team) along with the work itself. This whole activity is an adjunct to the normal work: it is the extra mile which lesser teams would not go, and for which your team will become famous.

Many products and services do not lend themselves to quality monitoring. These should be enhanced so that the quality becomes easily tracked. This may be a simple invitation for the 'customer' to comment, or it could be a full design modification to provide self-checking or an easy-testing routine. Any product whose quality cannot be tracked should naturally become a source of deep anxiety to the whole team – until a mechanism is devised.

In devising a mechanism for monitoring quality, many teams will produce a set of test procedures. As bugs emerge, new procedures should be added which specifically identify this problem and thereby check the solution. Even when the problem is solved the new procedures should *remain* in the test set; the problem may return (perhaps as a side effect of a subsequent modification) or the procedure may catch another. Essentially the test set should grow to cover all *known possibilities* of error and its application should, where possible, be automated.

One of the least-used sources of quality in design and production is documentation. This is frequently seen as the final inconvenience, sometimes even given to another group – yet the writing of such documentation can be used as an important vehicle for the clarification of ideas. It also protects the group from the loss of any single individual; the No.13 bus, or the head-hunter, can strike at any time.

Role change

As your team develop, your role as manager changes subtly. You become a cross between a priest and a rugby captain, providing the vision and the values while shouting like crazy from the centre of the field (the chutzpah). Although you retain the final say (that is your responsibility), the team begin to make decisions. The hardest part, as with all delegation, is accepting the group decision even though you disagree. You must never countermand a marginal decision. If you have to over-rule the team, it is imperative that you explain your reasons very clearly so that they understand the criteria; this will both justify your intervention and coach the team in (hopefully) good decision-making practices.

The Protector and Provider roles become more important as you are both buffer and interface between the team and the rest of the company: a buffer in that you protect the team from the vagaries of less enlightened managers who may resist these changes, an interface in that you keep the team informed about factors relevant to their decisions. Ultimately, the team will be delegating to you (!) tasks which only you, acting as manager, can perform on their behalf.

7.3 Quality for the Future

By applying the principles of quality to an established team, a manager can enjoy the benefits so actively sought by large corporations. The key is the attitude – and the insistence on the primacy of quality. As a manager, you have the power to define the ethos of your staff; by using quality as the focus, you also can accrue its riches.

If you want a different focus for a start perhaps you could try the following. Instead of *Watch the Manager*, this time the game is called: '*Follow your Product*'.

Step 1: establish clearly (write it down) what your team actually provide, that is, what products or services depend upon you. As before, these may be purely internal to the company with no interfaces to the outside world but do include any contacts you do have with the company's customers or suppliers, no matter how small.

Step 2: from your list, choose the product or service which is most significant to your customers (according to the criteria *you* select).

Step 3: now follow the product, both ways. A diagram like the one on the next page for 'Product Delta' (Δ) might help you to visualize this flow. Mark precisely the source of all the supplies (including data and information) which contribute to this product or service, and the destination and the subsequent use made of it by your customers. This is not a trivial task. It will require a lot of conversation and careful thought.

A Product Delta: Δ G

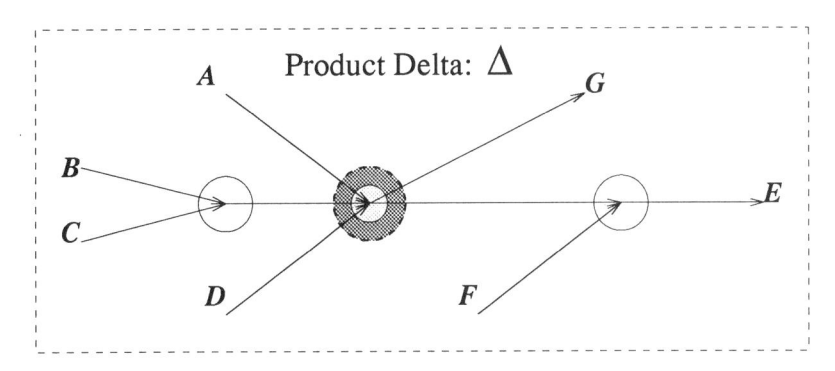

B
C
D F
E

You can adapt and adopt many different conventions to display this information; often they will be *ad hoc* to add clarity to specific problems. With Δ above, the product is the shaded circle and relies upon four inputs (A-D) and leads to two distinct outputs (E and G). The two other circles represent stages when distinct pieces are combined: B with C before becoming part of Δ, and F with Δ itself before it can be released in the final form as E. For instance, this diagram would make plain that your work depends upon the supply of F even though it is not identified as part of your Δ product.

Step 4: look at the interfaces (the arcs on the above diagram). For each one, identify an existing problem (possibly just an inconvenience) or a possible improvement. Look only at aspects of the interchange over which your team has control. If your output combines with another (as with F) then check for overlap or repetition of effort.

Step 5: choose the *two* most significant problems (your criteria) from the previous step and establish a mechanism *to monitor* these. Perform the monitoring for a short while to: 1) establish a base point, 2) determine if effort is merited.

Step 6: fix the worse problem (with the help of your team) and use the monitored improvements to demonstrate (and reinforce) your team's new quality.

Summary of Quality

What is Quality?
- The Customer — (basic survival)
- Reliability — (built-in permanence)
- People — (the team is king)
- Long Term — (managing the future)

Team Quality
- Get Started — (long-term process)
- Quick Kill — (success motivates)
- Build the Team — (build on each good idea)
- Mutual Coaching — (learning support)
- Statistics
  - quantify problem
  - tack progress
  - review → start again / celebrations

Project: AIM METHOD STATISTICS CRITERIA

Interfaces: the breeding ground for monsters

Become enthusiastic - a zealot - about quality

Ask your team for problems to solve

Check the interfaces for customer problems

Support your team's development

Always monitor the extent and progress of a problem

Chapter: 8
Conversation Management

No sir ... we had talk *enough but no* conversation, *there was nothing* discussed
(Samuel Johnson)

As a manager, you seek communication rather than chatter. Most conversations drift along; in business, this is wasteful. While there is a place for simple chatting (for instance, to establish a rapport) it should not be confused with effective communication. While you may aim to sound informal and relaxed, this is simply a technique to assist the communication.

The view given in previous chapters: that communication is only about 'the receipt' of your message, is a gross over simplification and applies only to the planning of formal, one-way, non-interactive, events. When you hold 'conversations', communication is far more complex. To ensure an efficient and effective conversation, there are three considerations:

- you must make your message understood
- you must receive/understand the intended message sent to you
- you should exert some control over the flow of the communication

Thus *you must learn to listen as well as to speak*. Those who dismiss this as a mere platitude are already demonstrating an indisposition to listening: the phrase may be trite, but the message is hugely significant to your effectiveness as a manager. If you do not explicitly develop the skill of listening, you may not hear the suggestion/information which could launch you to fame and fortune.

Communication is best achieved through simple planning and control; this chapter looks at approaches which might help you to do this, and at specific situations in your work where the conversation needs careful planning.

8.1 Ambiguity Avoidance

As a manager (concerned with getting things done) your view of words should be pragmatic rather than philosophical. Thus, words mean not what the dictionary says they do but rather what the speaker intended.

Suppose your manager gives to you an instruction which contains an ambiguity which neither of you notices and which results in you producing entirely the wrong product. Who is at fault? The answer must be: who cares? Your time has been wasted, the needed product is delayed (or dead); attributing blame may be a satisfying (or defensive) exercise but it does not address the problem. In everything you say or hear, you must look out for possible misunderstanding *and clarify* the ambiguity.

The greatest source of difficulty is that words often have different meanings depending upon context and/or culture. Thus, a 'dry' country lacks either water or alcohol; 'suspenders' keep up either stockings or trousers (pants); a 'funny' meeting is either humorous or disconcerting; a 'couple' is either a few or exactly two. If you recognize that there is a potential misunderstanding, you must stop the conversation and clarify.

A second problem is that some people simply make mistakes. Your job is not simply to spot ambiguities but also to counter inconsistencies. Thus if I now advocate that the wise manager should seek out (perhaps humorous) books on entomology, you could guess that I mean etymology. Often, when thinking through several alternatives, you can suffer a momentary confusion and say one of them while meaning another. There are good scientific reasons (to do with the associative nature of the brain) why this happens. You have to be aware of the potential problem and counter it.

Finally, of course, you may simply mishear. The omission of a simple word can be devastating. For instance, how long would you last as an explosives expert if you failed to hear a simple negative in: 'whatever happens next you must [not] cut the blue wi...'?

So, the problem is this: the word has multiple meanings, it might not be the one intended, and you may have misheard it in the first place – how do you know what the speaker meant?

Rule 1: play back for confirmation

Simple, you ask for confirmation. You say, 'Let me see if I understood correctly, you are saying that ...' and you *rephrase* what the speaker said. If this 'play back' version is acknowledged as being correct by the original speaker, then you have a greater degree of confidence in your own understanding. For any viewpoint/message/decision, there should be a clear, concise and verified statement of what was said; without this someone will get it wrong.

Rule 2: write back for confidence

But do not stop there. If your time and effort depend upon it, you should write it down and send it to everyone involved as a double check. This has several advantages:

- Further clarification – is this what you thought we agreed?
- Consistency check – the act of writing may highlight defects/omissions
- A formal stage – a statement of the accepted position provides a springboard for action
- Evidence – hindsight blurs previous ignorance and people often fail to recall their previous errors

Rule 3: give background for context

When others are speaking, you should deliberately ask questions to establish the context in which they are thinking. When speaking yourself, you can counter for possible problems by adding information, and so provide a broader context in which your words can be understood. Thus, there is less scope for alternative interpretations since fewer are consistent.

Of course, giving full information has other benefits. Suppose you are booking travel tickets. If you call the agent and ask for a specific ticket on a specific flight on a specific route on a specific day, then that is what you will get. If, instead, you give the context (a conference from Tuesday at 1pm, and returning for baby Sarah's birthday party on Thursday evening), the agent may well offer you a better ticket at a more convenient time by a preferable route (and a complimentary teddy bear for little Sarah). Without the wider context, the agent has no opportunity to apply his/her expertise or solicit your further custom through gestures of quality service and customer care. In general, the wider context may enable someone not only to understand better, but also to contribute insight and experience in the response.

> *To Practise 8.1:* Using your common sense, devise a formula to reduce the possibility of others misunderstanding what you say.

8.2 Practical Points

As with all effective communication, you should decide (in advance) on the purpose of the conversation and on a plan for achieving it. There is no alternative to this. Some people are proficient at 'thinking on their feet' – but this is generally because they already have clear understanding of the context and of their own goals. You have to plan; however, the following are a few techniques to help the conversation along.

Assertiveness

The definition of *to assert* is: 'to declare; state clearly'. This is your aim. If people argue against you, even lose their temper, you should be quietly assertive. Much has been written to preach this simple fact and commonly the final message is a three-fold plan of action:

- acknowledge what is being said by showing an understanding of the position, or by simply replaying it (a polite way of saying 'I heard you already')
- state your own point of view clearly and concisely with perhaps a little supporting evidence
- state what you want to happen next (move it forward)

Thus we have something like: 'yes, I see why you need the report by tomorrow; however, I have no time today to prepare the document because I am in a meeting with a customer this afternoon. Either I could give you the raw data and you could work on it yourself, or you could make do with the interim report from last week.'

You will have to make many personal judgement calls when being assertive. There will certainly be times when a bit of quiet force will win the day but there will be times when this will get nowhere, particularly with more senior (and unenlightened) management. In the latter case, you must agree to abide by the decision of the senior manager but you should make your objection (and reasons) clearly known. For yourself, always be aware that your subordinates might be right when they disagree with you and if events prove them so, acknowledge that fact gracefully.

> *To Practise 8.2:* Try it. Next time you witness a disagreement, frame in your own mind how one combatant might be assertive: 'I see you think this, however I believe this, we should do this'.

Confrontations

When you have a difficult encounter, be professional; do not lose your self-control because, simply, it is of no use. Some managers believe that it is useful for 'discipline' to keep staff a little nervous. Thus, these managers are slightly volatile and will be willing 'to let them have it' when the situation demands. If you do this, you must be consistent *and fair* so that your staff know where they stand. If you deliberately lose your temper for effect, then that is your decision – however, you must never lose control.

Insults are ineffective. If you call people names, then they are unlikely to actually *listen* to what you have to say; in the short term you may feel some relief at 'getting it off your chest', but in the long run you are merely perpetuating the problem since you are not addressing it. This is common sense. There are two implications. Firstly, even under pressure, you have to remember this. Secondly, what you consider fair comment may be insulting to another – and the same problem emerges. Before you say *anything*, stop, establish what you want as the outcome, plan how to achieve this, and then speak.

Finally, if you are going to criticize or discipline someone, always assume that you have misunderstood the situation and ask questions first which check the facts. This simple courtesy will save you from much embarrassment.

Seeking Information

There are two ways of phrasing any question: one way (the closed question) is likely to lead to a simple grunt in reply (yes, no, maybe), the second way (the open question) will hand over the speaking role to someone else and force him/her to say something a little more informative.

Suppose you conduct a review of a recently-finished (?) project with Arnold (remember Arnold?) and it goes something like this:

'Have you finished project X, Arnold?'

'Yes'

'Is everything written up?'

'Nearly'

'So there is documentation left to do?'

'Some'

'Will it take you long?'

'No, not long'

116   Starting to Manage

Before your fingers start twitching to place themselves around Arnold's neck, consider that your questions are not actually helping the flow of information. The same flow of questions in an *open* format would be: What is left to do of project X? What about the documentation? When will that be completely finished? Try answering yes or no to those questions.

Open questions are extremely easy to formulate. You establish in your own mind the topic/aim of the question and then you start the sentence with the words:

> WHAT – WHEN – WHICH – WHY – WHERE – HOW

> *To Practise 8.3:* Write down these simple words on a discrete piece of paper and put it at the side of your desk. For the next three days, try to make every question an open question.

Let others speak
Of course, there is more to a conversation (managed or otherwise) than the flow of information. You may also have to win that information by winning the attention and confidence of the other person. Consider this problem: you need assistance in deciding a certain issue, and you suspect that Arnold may have some ideas.

First of all, who needs to do the talking? Arnold. Who therefore needs to keep quiet? You do. What then is your aim in the conversation? To stimulate Arnold to expound, and to focus his train of thought.

There are many forms of flattery – the most effective is to give people your interest. To get Arnold to give you all his knowledge, you must give him all your attention; talk to him about *his* view on the subject. Ask questions: What do you think about that idea? Have you ever met this problem before? How would you tackle this situation?

Silence is effective – and much under-used. People are nervous of silence and try to fill it. You can use this if you are seeking information. You ask the question, you lean back, the person answers, you nod and smile, you keep quiet, and the person continues with more detail simply to fill your silence.

To start
At the beginning of a conversation, you have to gain people's attention or they may miss the significant point. You do not need a dramatic opening, merely a pause. You make some greeting and then stop until you have their attention (especially eye contact). Always try to have a friendly expression ready.

To Practise 8.4: For the next week, cause every shop assistant that serves you to remember you in particular (for some positive, friendly reason).

To finish

At the end of a conversation, you have to give people a clear understanding of the outcome. For instance, if there has been a decision, restate it clearly (just to be sure) in terms of what should happen and by when; if you have been asking questions, summarize the significant aspects of what you have learnt.

8.3 Telephony or Cacophony?

As a first example of a managed conversation, consider that happy distraction at the side of your desk, and decide exactly what you want to do with it. For some, the ring/trill/bleat of the telephone can signal the end of concentration and controlled schedules. While it should be a tool for coordination over distance, it is more often the fool's alternative to the chat around the coffee machine – and since it sits on your desk, you are vulnerable. You must manage this tool.

.... and one day, children, you will all be mobile

When you make a telephone call, you do so with a definite purpose. The best approach is to write this down beforehand. A simple note, with each point you need to raise, sitting beside the phone, will enable you to follow your own agenda without omissions or deviation. Never start a call without a note of your intention.

You need to gain the attention of the person you are calling. Often, the phone call does interrupt a train of thought, or a delicate calculation, and the recipient is initially distracted. Since you cannot see the other end of the phone, the recipient will probably continue doodling, or scribbling, or tapping the keyboard, as you speak. You must compensate. If you do not, then your call will be far less effective. One way to start is by asking if it is convenient to speak now. This simple courtesy will either focus the recipient to your call (responding with courtesy) or enable him/her to defer until it is mutually convenient. One attention grabber is to state clearly and concisely what the call is about at the very beginning (i.e. read out your agenda/note). To speed things along, make sure that you preface the conversation with any useful background (for instance, your name and company).

> Always plan your first line before dialling

It is important that you provide as much relevant information as possible. For instance, if you are calling long distance or in difficult circumstances, tell the switchboard: 'Good morning, my name is Gerard Blair and I'm calling from a converted yak shack in Outer Mongolia, please may I speak to ...'. Common sense will tell you if you need special attention, but *you* have to tell the person on the other end of the phone.

When someone phones you, there are two things you need to consider:

- how long does this call merit
- what information do *you* need (particularly to establish the context)

To speed things along, establish the context of the call at the beginning and the probable agenda – then start it rolling. The pleasantries should be limited to just that – if the caller continues to chat, apologize and say simply that you can only spare a couple of minutes, how can you help?

> *To Practise 8.5:* Suppose you want to ask Arnold for an update on his project. *Write down* exactly what you need to know, plan your opening line (so that he knows exactly what you want), plan how to end (perhaps to encourage him), and call.

Sometimes, your time management may dictate that you do not answer the phone. This is a dangerous policy, however, since the call might be urgent, the caller may be offering you promotion, or a person with regular phone habits may always find you unavailable. If you decide to ignore the phone, you must establish two safe-guards: 1) get the calls rerouted to a secretary who will take a full message (you will need to specify this delegated task clearly), and 2) ensure that your team know this trick and will come to find you if they need to. If you deal with the messages on a frequent basis, no caller will feel too offended; if you let them lapse, the caller may never return and you may lose.

8.4 The Selection Interview

Another example of a structured conversation is the job selection interview. Here you are given a short space of time in which to judge a candidate. As with every conversation, you must decide beforehand exactly what you want to achieve and how best to go about it.

> *To Practise 8.6:* Pause for a moment and consider exactly what you do want of someone who will fill your next vacant post.

There are two starting points for a successful interview:

- a specified list of required and desired abilities
- the existing information on the candidate

As an interviewer, your job is to decide whether the candidate has the abilities which the job requires.

Errors

There is a great tradition of interviewing tricks and techniques. Since so much mystery and secrecy surrounds job-selection procedures, what people believe to be effective is seldom (if ever) actually tested against the outcome. For one thing, no one knows how well the rejected candidate would have performed in the job, and few remember (or knew) why the accepted candidate was actually chosen. You must judge all the old stories in terms of your own objectives for the conversation; if they do not help – ignore them.

Let us deal with two common prejudices (concerning factors affecting staff turnover) and examine alternative interpretations.

Take the assumption that young, newly-married women are likely to leave quickly and have a baby. Point one, married couples are inherently less mobile than a single person and so less likely to leave the area (thus reducing the range of alternative employment); point two, maternity rights actually encourage women to remain with a company for a lengthy period of time *if* having a baby is in fact their objective.

Take the assumption that people in their early fifties are past their sell-by-date. Point one, they have a lot of experience to offer; point two, they are less likely than a younger candidate to want further change because of retirement benefits.

Either of these two groups of people is likely to stay longer with the company than the traditionally favoured, single young male. And while these prejudices continue, both groups are likely to display loyalty to any manager who is more enlightened.

The point is that (very) little inference can be drawn from a candidate's gender or age, and the most common deductions are often illogical and merely reflect conventional prejudice. Not only is it illegal to use such criteria, it is also erroneous; as a manager, you must base your judgement on far more solid ground.

Another source of error is the *halo effect*: something in the candidate is so striking that your judgement of every other criterion is affected. For instance, the candidate may be physically attractive (or repulsive), he/she may share your fanaticism for philately, you may both have gone to the same school. Now these (or rather some of these) do perhaps provide you with an insight into the person's character and background; there can be a case for 'better the devil you recognize'; but there is no reason for letting this affect your judgement on the real issues.

The most ludicrous criterion, however, is to judge someone according to their *personality*. Apply common sense: what is personality, can you define the personality traits best suited to the vacant position, are you able to test for the existence of these, might the (wise) candidate not guess what you want and simply act the part? Your company may use psychometric analysis to establish personality traits – and you can judge what weight to give to these results – but in the interview you conduct, stick to what *you* can validly determine.

Match making
To select a candidate you need objective criteria. Take a good look at the job and responsibilities, and write them down. For each category, highlight those parts of the candidate's particulars which are relevant so that you know to probe these sections further, and note down any omissions so that you can discuss these with the candidate. Finally, look carefully at the candidate's particulars to decide whether there is any relevant information which might have been overstated or omitted ('why did you leave McBlair's so soon after joining?') so that you can clarify these points during the conversation.

That is it. There is no more. All you can gain from an interview is information pertaining to the facts you judge to be important.

So if you are interested in the extent of the candidate's actual involvement in a specific project (to judge the supposed technical experience thereby gained), say: 'Please would you describe exactly what you did as part of project Y?' If you need to judge the education of a computer programmer, weed out the amateurs by asking a technical question: 'how is a hash-table designed?' If you want information about the candidate's management skills, ask: 'How many people reported to you at Z?' Deduce the information you need, devise a question to gain it, avoid making assumptions without facts.

> *To Practise 8.7:* Consider what your own best talents are and how someone else might discover them through asking questions. What 'hints' might you supply in an application form or in a short 'personal statement'?

8.5 Meeting Management (I) – Preparation

In any organization, 'meetings' are a vital part of the organization of work and the flow of information. They act as a mechanism for gathering together resources and pooling then towards a common objective. They are disliked and mocked because they are usually futile, boring, time-wasting, dull, and inconvenient, with nothing for most people to do except doodle while some opinionated smart-arse extols the virtues of his/her last great (misunderstood) half-baked idea. Your challenge, as a *great* manager, is to break this mould and to make your meetings effective. As with every other managed activity, meetings should be planned beforehand, monitored during, and reviewed afterward.

A meeting is the ultimate form of managed conversation; as a manager, you can organize the information and structure of the meeting to support the effective communication of the participants. Some of the ideas below may seem a little too precise for an easy going, relaxed, semi-informal team atmosphere – but if you manage to gain a reputation for holding decisive, effective meetings, then people will value this efficiency and prepare professionally so that their contribution will be heard.

Should you cancel?
As with all conversations, you must first ask: 'Is it worth your time?' If the meeting involves the exchange of views and the communication of the current status of related projects, then you should be generous; but you should always consider cancelling a meeting which has little tangible value.

Who should attend?
You must be strict. A meeting loses its effectiveness if too many people are involved; so if someone has no useful function, explain this and suggest that they do not come. Note, they may disagree with your assessment, in which case they should attend (since they may know something you do not); however, most people are happy to be released from yet another meeting.

How long?
It may seem difficult to predict the length of a discussion – but you must. Discussions tend to fill the available time which means that if the meeting is open-ended, it will drift on forever. You should stipulate a time for the end of the meeting so that everyone knows and can plan the rest of the day with confidence.

It is wise to make this expectation known to all involved well in advance and to remind them at the beginning of the meeting. There is often a tendency to view meetings as a little relaxation since no one person has to be active throughout. You can redress this view by stressing the time-scale and thus forcing the pace of the discussion: 'this is what we have to achieve, this is how long we have to do it'.

If some unexpected point arises during the meeting, you should remember that, since it is unexpected: 1) you might not have the right people present, 2) those there may not have the necessary information, and 3) a little thought might save a lot of discussion. If the new discussion looks likely to be more than a few moments, stop it and deal with the agreed agenda. The new topic should then be dealt with at another 'planned' meeting.

Agenda
The purpose of an agenda is to inform participants of the subject of the meeting in advance, and to structure the discussion at the meeting itself. To inform people beforehand, and to solicit ideas, you should circulate a draft agenda and ask for notice of any other business. Still before the meeting, you should then send the revised agenda with enough time for people to prepare their contributions. If someone will be providing information at the meeting, make this *explicitly* clear so that there is no confusion.

To keep your team informed, it is worth displaying the agenda for all to see. Then if non-attendees do wish to contribute, they can make their input known to those who are going. If you frame each agenda item in such a way that there is an answer, then after the meeting you can display the results as bullet points to each question. This can then be used as a simple monitor of the meeting's effectiveness (i.e. did it achieve its goals?).

BUILDING TOGETHER

This is a very important point, so here it comes again. The agenda states the purpose of each section of the meeting. There will be an outcome from each section. If that outcome is so complex that it cannot be summarized in a few points, then it was probably too complex to be assimilated by the participants. The understanding of the meeting should be sufficiently precise that it can be summarized in short form – so display that summary for all other interested parties to see. This form of display will emphasize to all that meetings are about achieving defined goals – this will help you to continue running efficient meetings in the future.

Housekeeping
The most detrimental start imaginable to a meeting is for the manager to arrive and find the participants sitting in the corridor, the door locked, the key on holiday with the janitor and no option other than to lead the pack off on a random search for other rooms. There are basic requirements such as booking the room, checking the equipment, posting the paperwork. You are responsible – delegate it effectively.

> *To Practise 8.8:* After the next meeting you attend, consider how its effectiveness might have been improved by attention to the suggestions in this section.

8.6 Meeting Management (II) – Conducting

Whether you actually sit as the Chair or simply lead from the side-lines, as the manager you must provide the necessary support to coordinate the contributions of the participants. The degree of control which you exercise over the meeting will vary throughout; if you get the structure right at the beginning, a meeting can effectively run itself, especially if the participants know each other well. In a team, your role may be partially undertaken by others; but if not, you must manage.

Maintaining communication

Your most important tools are:

- Clarification – always clarify: the purpose of the meeting, the time allowed, the rules to be observed (if agreed) by everyone.

- Summary – at each stage of the proceedings, you should summarize the current position and progress: this is what we have achieved/agreed, this is where we have reached.

- Focus on stated goals – at each divergence or pause, re-focus the proceedings on the original goals.

Code of conduct

In any meeting, it is possible to begin the proceedings by establishing a code of conduct, often by merely stating it and asking for any objections (which will only be accepted if a demonstrably better system is proposed). Thus if the group contains opinionated wind-bags, you might all agree at the onset to limit contributions to two minutes (which focuses the mind admirably). You can then impose this with the full backing of the whole group.

Matching method to purpose

The (stated) purpose of a meeting may suggest to you a specific way of conducting the event, and each section might be conducted differently. For instance, if the purpose is:

- to convey information, the meeting might begin with a formal presentation followed by questions

- to seek information, the meeting might start with a short (clear) statement of the topic/problem and then an open discussion supported by notes on a display, or a formal brainstorming session

- to make a decision, the meeting might review the background and options, *establish the criteria* to be applied, agree who should make the decision and how, and then do it

- to ratify/explain decisions, etc, etc

As always, once you have paused to ask yourself the questions: 'what is the purpose of the meeting?' and 'how can it be most effectively achieved?'; your common sense will then suggest a working method to expedite the proceedings. You just have deliberately to pause. Manage the process of the meeting and the meeting will work.

Support

The success of a meeting will often depend upon the confidence with which the individuals participate. Thus all ideas should be welcome. No one should be laughed at or dismissed ('laughed with' is good, 'laughed at' is destructive). This means that even bad ideas should be treated seriously – and at least merit a specific reason for not being pursued further. Not only is this supportive to the speaker, it could also be that a good idea has been misunderstood and would be lost if merely rejected. Basically, people should be able to make naive contributions without being made to feel stupid, otherwise you may never hear the best ideas of all.

Avoid direct criticism of any person. For instance, if someone has not come prepared then that fault is obvious to all. If you leave the criticism as being simply that implicit in the peer pressure, then it is diffuse and general; if you explicitly rebuke that person, then it is personal and from you (which may raise unnecessary conflict). You should merely seek an undertaking for the missing preparation to be done: 'we need to know this before we can proceed, could you circulate it to us by tomorrow lunch?'. If you think that an explicit rebuke is necessary, do it privately outside of the meeting (and see chapter 9).

Discussions are often a journey and each person is very attached to the steps they provide, so always try to build upon the ideas expressed before: 'taking what Alice said earlier, we could apply the same idea to ...'

If you are in the authority position, you must be aware that your attitude can affect the whole group. Thus, you should be seen to be attentive, and actively listening to the contributions (each and every one of them).

Spare a little contribution for your manager

If you are trying to encourage the shyer members, be supportive of contributions: 'that is a good point'. Also, such people should be asked direct (open) questions during any discussion where they have knowledge or experience: 'Arnold, you know something about this, what do you think?'

Planning contributions

Meetings, and large discussions in general, can be enhanced by taking scribbled notes, particularly of questions you need to ask as they occur to you. If you have a contribution to make, sketch it lightly on your note paper beforehand (as bullet points) so that you order your thoughts before you open your mouth. When you make a contribution to the discussion, think it through first and then speak clearly and concisely.

Responding to problems

The rest of this section is devoted to ideas about how you might deal with the various problems associated with the volatile world of meetings. Some are best undertaken by the designated Chair; but if he/she is ineffective, or if no one has been appointed, you should feel free to help any meeting to progress. After all, why should you allow your time to be wasted?

- If a participant strays from the agenda item, call him/her back: 'We should deal with that separately. What do you feel about the issue X?'
- If the speaker begins to ramble, wait until an inhalation of breath and jump in: 'Yes, I understand that such and such, does anyone disagree?'
- If a point is too woolly or too vague ask for greater clarity: 'What exactly do you have in mind?'
- If someone interrupts someone else (other than a rambler), suggest that 'We should hear your contribution after Arnold has finished.'
- If people chat, you might either simply state your difficulty in hearing/concentrating on the real speaker or ask them a direct question: 'What do you think about that point?'
- If someone gestures disagreement with the speaker (e.g. by a grimace), then make sure they are brought into the discussion next: 'What do you think Arnold?'
- If you do not understand, say so: 'I do not understand that, would you explain it a little more?' or 'Do you mean X or Y?'
- If there is an error, look for a good point first: 'I see how that would work if X Y Z, but what would happen if A B C?'
- If you disagree, be *very* specific: 'I disagree *because* ...'

> *To Practise 8.9:* In the next few meetings, note down any difficulties which arise and afterwards think through ways of intervening. You might even raise these problems with the whole group before the next meeting (impersonally) and ask for their suggestions – this at least makes them aware.

8.7 Communication

The tower of Babel collapsed because people could no longer communicate; their speech became so different that no one could understand another. You need to communicate to coordinate your own work and that of others. Without explicit effort your conversation will lack communication and so your work too will collapse though misunderstanding and error. The key is to treat a conversation as you would any other managed activity: by establishing an aim, planning what to do, and checking afterwards that you have achieved that aim. Only in this way can you work effectively with others in building through common effort.

As always, your main learning will come through deliberately watching others and then trying out your own ideas. *Watch the Manager* is now transformed into *Listen to the Manager*. Because you are now aware of the true role of conversation at work, you will be able to recognize the other managers who are already practised at this. Whenever you talk with, or observe, such a person – try to guess the intended agenda, watch their techniques for directing the conversation, and *note down* any ideas you think might help you. This is particularly useful in the context of meeting management.

To manage your telephone calls, it is worth actually keeping track of the time. If you are calling someone (and have your written agenda) note down how long each item takes and estimate how much time is wasted on irrelevancies. If you are being called, consider the speed and clarity with which the caller establishes the context and moves through his/her own agenda.

To prepare yourself better for conducting selection interviews, take a closer look at your existing team and decide for each member what skill, ability, or characteristic makes that person a 'good' member of the team, and then how you would discover this trait at an interview. The answer must lie either in the documentation submitted beforehand or in the questions you ask at interview; these are your only tools.

Summary of Conversations

Avoid misunderstandings	Assertiveness
PLAY BACK	I understand you
WRITE BACK	I believe that
GIVE BACKground	We should
Maintain control	Quiet attention

Open questions:
　　what - when - which - why - where - how

Telephone
　　Write out your agenda
　　Plan your first line
　　Establish Context

Job Selection
　　Determine job requirements
　　Examine the documentation
　　Question to see if candidate meets the objective requirements

Meetings
　　Who - what - how long
　　Manage the agenda
　　Provide support for all contributions

Chapter: 9
People

Where there is no vision, the people perish
(Proverbs 29:18)

When you are struggling with deadlines or dealing with delicate decisions, the last thing you want to deal with is 'people'. When the fight is really on and the battle is undecided, you want your team to act co-operatively, quickly, rationally; you do not want a disgruntled worker bitching about life, you do not want a worker who avoids work, you do not want your key worker being tired all day because the neighbours fight all night. But this is what happens, and as a manager you have to deal with it. Few 'people problems' can be solved quickly, some are totally beyond your control and can only be contained; but you do have influence over many factors which affect your people and so it is your responsibility to ensure that your influence is a positive one.

You can only underestimate the impact which you personally have upon the habits and effectiveness of your group. As the manager of a team, you have the authority to sanction, encourage or restrict most aspects of their working day, and this places you in a position of power – and responsibility. This chapter looks briefly at your behaviour and at what motivates people, because by understanding these you can adapt yourself and the work environment so that your team and the company are both enriched. Since human psychology is a vast and complex subject, we will not even pretend to explain it. Instead, we will look at a simple model of behaviour and a systematic approach to analysing how you can exert your influence to help your team to work.

9.1 Behaviour

Consider your behaviour. Consider the effect you would have if every morning after coffee you walked over to Arnold's desk and told him what he was doing wrong. Would Arnold feel pleased at your attention? Would he look forward to these little chats? Would he prepare simple questions to clarify aspects of his work? Or would he develop a Pavlovian hatred for coffee and be busy elsewhere whenever you pass by? Of course you would never be so destructive – provided you thought about it. And you must, for many seemingly simple habits can have a huge impact upon your team.

Take another example: suppose (as a good supportive manager) you often give public praise for the independence and initiative displayed in your team, and at the same time (as a busy manager) you respond brusquely to questions and interruptions; think about it, what will happen? Probably your team will leave you alone. They will not raise problems (you will be left in the dark), they will not question your instructions (ambiguities will remain), they will struggle on bravely (and feel unsupported). Your simple behaviour may result in a quagmire of errors, misdirected activity and utter frustration. So if you do want to hear about problems, tell the team so and react positively when they bring you their problems in time rather than too late.

This concern for behaviour does not imply that you should wander around with evangelical zeal or the determined smile of a presidential hopeful; it means that your behaviour is important and that you should take care to manage its impact upon the atmosphere and motivation of the team. If you have a positive outlook, your team will also. If you are supportive, your team will respond and grow. If you remain calm in a crisis, then so may your team; if you throw a fit and run around like a headless chicken, so will they.

9.2 Motivation

When thinking about motivation it is important to take the long-term view. What you need is a sustainable approach to maintain enthusiasm and commitment from your team. This is not easy; but it is essential to your effectiveness.

Illuminating work on motivation was undertaken by Frederick Herzberg in the 1950s when he formulated the 'Motivation-Hygiene' theory. Herzberg identified several factors, such as salary levels, working conditions and company policy, which demotivated (by being poor) rather that motivated (by being good). For example, once a fair level of pay is established, money ceases to be a significant motivator for long-term performance. Herzberg called these the 'Hygiene' factors to apply the analogy that if the washrooms are kept clean, no one cares if they are scrubbed even harder. The point is that you cannot enhance your team's performance using the Hygiene factors – which is fortunate since few managers actually have creative control over company organization or remuneration packages. What you can influence is the local environment and particularly the way in which you interact with your team.

TRUE REWARDS

Achievement   *Advancement*

The Work

Recognition   *Responsibility*

The positive motivators identified by Herzberg are: achievement, recognition, the work itself, advancement and responsibility. These are what your team need; loads-o-money is nice but not nearly as good as being valued and trusted.

Achievement
As the manager, you set the targets – and in selecting these targets, you have a dramatic effect upon your team's sense of achievement. The targets should be difficult but achievable; if you make them too hard, the team will feel failure; if too easy, the team feel little. Ideally, you should provide a series of targets which are easily recognized as stages towards the ultimate completion of the task. Thus progress is punctuated and celebrated with small but marked achievements. If you stretch your staff, they know you know they can meet that challenge.

Recognition
Recognition is about feeling appreciated. It is knowing that what you do is seen and noted, preferably by the whole team as well as by you, the manager. In opposite terms, if people do something well and then feel it is ignored – they will not bother to do it as well next time (because 'no one cares'). There should be a place in your team's organization for mutual recognition. Each should know what the others are doing and feel able/encouraged to offer support and suggestions.

The feedback you give your team about their work is fundamental to their motivation. Your staff need to know where they stand, and how they are performing against your (reasonable) expectations. You can achieve this through a structured review system, but such systems often become banal formalities with little or no communication. The best time to give feedback is when the event occurs. Since it can impact greatly, the feedback should be honest, simple, and always constructive. If in doubt, follow the simple formula – you should:

- highlight something good
- point out what needs improving
- suggest how to improve

You must always look for something positive to say, if only to offer some recognition of the effort which has been put into the work. When talking about improvements, be specific: this is what is wrong, this is what I want/need, this is how you should work towards it. Never say anything as unhelpful or uninformative as 'do better' or 'shape up' – if you cannot be specific and say how, then keep quiet. While your team will soon realize that this IS a formula, they will still enjoy the benefits of the information (and training). You must not stint in praise of good work. If you do not acknowledge it, it may not be repeated simply because no one knew you approved.

Following the same formula, the team should also have an understanding of your views on their work in general. They should know:

- what they do well – be positive
- what needs improving – be constructive
- what is expected of them in the future – something to aim at

> *To Practise 9.1:* And while this is common sense, ask yourself how many on your team know these things, right now? Perhaps more importantly, do *you* know? For each of your team, *write down* an example of his/her work in each of these three categories?

The Work Itself

The work itself should be interesting and challenging. Interesting because this makes your staff actually engage their attention; challenging because this maintains their interest and provides a sense of personal achievement when the job is done. But few managers have only interesting, challenging work to distribute: there is always the boring and mundane to be done. This is a management problem for you to solve. You must actually consider how interesting (to the people who receive them) are the tasks you assign, and how to deal with the boring ones. Here are two suggestions.

First, make sure that everyone (including yourself) has a share of the interesting and of the dull. This is helped by the fact that what is dull to some might be new and fascinating to others – so match tasks to people, and share the worst tasks around. For instance, taking minutes in meetings is dull on a weekly basis but quite interesting/educational once every six weeks (and also heightens a sense of responsibility), so let everyone in the group take turns.

Second, if the task is dull perhaps the same objective could be achieved by another method – devised by the person given the task. This turns dull into challenging, adds responsibility, and might even improve the efficiency of the team.

Advancement

There are two types of advancement: the long-term issues of promotion, salary rises, job prospects; and the short-term issues (which you control) of increased responsibility, the acquisition of new skills, broader experience. Your team members will be looking for the former, you have to provide the latter and convince them that these are the necessary (and possibly sufficient) steps for the eventual advancement they seek. As a manager, you must design the work assignments so that each member of the team feels: 'I'm getting on, I'm getting there'.

Responsibility

Of all of Herzberg's positive motivators, responsibility is the most lasting. One reason is that gaining responsibility is itself seen as an advancement which gives rise to a sense of achievement and can also improve the work itself: a multiple motivator! Assigning responsibility is a difficult judgement. If the person is confident or not capable enough, you will be responsible for the resulting failure. Chapter 6 (on delegation) should be read with care. However, you should always delegate the maximum responsibility that each person can handle otherwise he/she will be under-used. Your maxim then should always be: *delegate or demotivate*.

> *To Practise 9.2:* Consider yourself and your current position. For the five positive motivators, *write down* the extent to which each affects your own personal motivation. For the motivator which is least influential at the moment, devise a strategy to make it more effective.

9.3 People Problems

With this slight understanding of motivation, we are now going to look at a simple system for addressing people-problems. It is a step-by-step procedure which avoids complex psychological models (which few managers can/should handle) and which focuses upon tangible (and so controllable) quantities.

One of the most attractive features of this system is that it does not rely exclusively upon the exercising of authority. People respond because they want to, not because they are told. Since you do not need to have authority, you can apply the same techniques to deal with people over whom you have none; for instance, your own manager.

One word of warning: this technique is often referred to as *Behavioural Modification* and many people balk at the connotations of management-directed mind control. Do not worry. We are simply recognizing that staff behaviour IS modified by the work environment and by your influence upon it. The technique is merely a method for analysing that influence to ensure that it is positive and focusing it to best use.

The traditional approach to Behavioural Modification

In any group of people there are bound to be problems – as a manager, you have to solve or at least contain them. You ignore them at your peril. If you deal with them, you can enhance the performance of your whole team. The following is a six stage procedure for addressing these 'opportunities'.

Stage 1: specify
Stage 1 is to specify *a definite* problem. The way one thinks of people-problems initially is usually in terms of broad generalities or 'labels'. For instance, they might say: 'Arnold is just lazy' or 'Brenda is a bad-tempered pedant'. On the one hand, these descriptions do express your frustration; on the other hand they are totally unhelpful and do not move you forward to a solution.

The underlying philosophy of Behavioural Modification is that you should concentrate only upon actual, tangible behaviours over which you have influence. You have to look for specific instances of behaviour which have led you to your general view – and then address these. For instance 'Arnold is just lazy' should be transformed into 'Arnold is normally late with his weekly report and achieves less than Alice does in any one week'. Thus you have a starting point and *something which can be measured*.

When performing Behavioural Modification, it is best to work on one behaviour at a time. Firstly, this simplifies the analysis. Secondly, when you address one problem, other related problems are often also affected, and the multiple effects of multiple modifications become impossible to predict or control.

Thus you must first describe your problem, remove all general 'labels', and focus upon only one, concrete, quantifiable behaviour which you wish the change. No generalities, only a specific, observable behaviour.

Stage 2: monitor
Before proceeding, it is worth checking that the problem is real – some 'problems' are more appearance than substance, some are not worth your time or effort. So, stage 2 is to monitor the identified problem to check that it is real and to seek simple explanations. For instance, Arnold might still be helping someone with his old job. Since the problem is specified as something which can be measured, measure it. This will show you the extent of the problem and give you a base-line against which to judge improvements.

Stage 3: discuss
Stage 3 is often missed – ask Arnold for a solution. This sort of interview can be quite difficult because you run the danger of making personal criticism. Now, you may feel that Arnold deserves criticism, but does it actually help? Your objective is to get Arnold to work well, not to indulge in tyranny. If you make it personal, Arnold will be defensive. He will either deny the problem, blame someone else, blame the weather, tell you that he

knows best or some combination of the above. If, on the other hand, you present the situation in terms of the specific events, you can focus upon Arnold's own view of the problem (why is this happening?) and Arnold's own solution (what can Arnold do about it – can you help?).

Stage 3 will sometimes be sufficient. If Arnold had thought his behaviour would pass unnoticed, he now knows differently. If Arnold had not realized there was a problem, he might might now be able to solve it. Often the demonstration that you are interested in Arnold's work will be enough to make him improve. By offering Arnold the responsibility for solving his own problem, you can actually motivate him and gain from his experience of the problem. For instance, he might even address a wider issue and suggest an improved reporting system, or a short training course to deal with a technical short-coming. Never assume that you know better, always ask first – then if no solutions are forthcoming, proceed to ...

Stage 4: analyse
Stage 4 is the analysis stage and is based upon a simple model: every behaviour is preceded by a trigger, and is followed by a consequence or payoff. Thus baby is hungry (trigger), baby wails (behaviour), baby gets fed (payoff); or the report is due today (trigger), Arnold goes for coffee 'to think about it' (behaviour), Arnold has a relaxing afternoon (payoff).

The main point is that a person's behaviour is reinforced if the resulting payoff (or reward) is pleasant or beneficial for that person. This is known as positive feedback. Sometimes, behaviour results in unpleasant or detrimental payoffs. This is negative feedback and the behaviour will tend to diminish. For example, if every time Arnold informs his boss Diane about a schedule change (behaviour), Diane vents her annoyance on Arnold (payoff), then Arnold will be less inclined to approach Diane with information in the future. In ancient Greece the bearer of bad news was often executed, which must have severely hampered communications.

The desired situation at work is, therefore, that good behaviour leads to a positive payoff which reinforces the good behaviour by positive feedback, and the bad behaviour leads to a negative payoff which deters the bad behaviour by negative feedback.

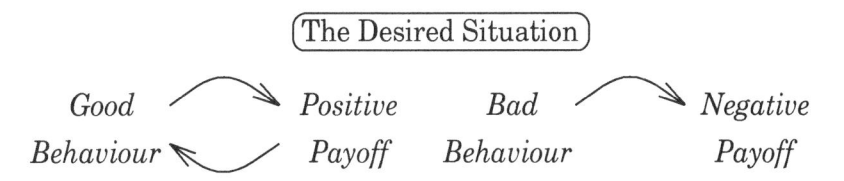

The Desired Situation

Good Behaviour ⇄ Positive Payoff   Bad Behaviour → Negative Payoff

The problems arise when the work environment and practices discourage good behaviour and encourage bad behaviour.

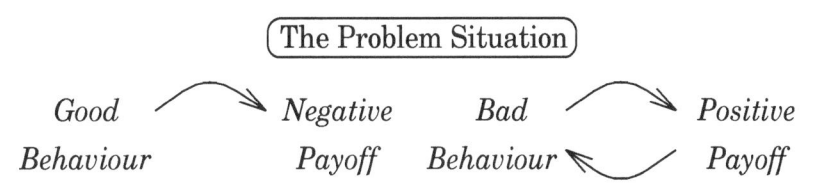

The Problem Situation

Good Behaviour → Negative Payoff   Bad Behaviour ⇄ Positive Payoff

The objective of the analysis stage is to look for all negative payoffs to good behaviour (which deter virtue) and all positive payoffs to bad behaviour (which encourage evil). In this way, you can discover why the current (undesirable) behaviour exists.

> *To Practise 9.3:* Consider your own behaviour. Can you isolate an example of good behaviour in your staff which is blocked by the negative feedback they receive from you?

Stage 5: modify payoffs

Once you have analysed the problem, stage 5 is to find a solution. With most people-problems at work, you will find that the 'bad' behaviour is reinforced by positive feedback. There are two solutions:

- modify the existing positive payoff – either by removing it or by adding a negative payoff
- create a new positive payoff for the alternative, desired 'good' behaviour.

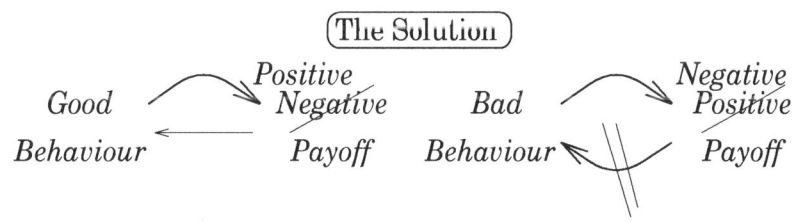

The Solution

Good Behaviour ← Positive / Negative Payoff   Bad Behaviour ⇄ Negative / Positive Payoff

In the long term, the latter is preferable since it is better for motivation to offer encouragement rather than reprimand; optimally you should implement both.

> *To Practise 9.4:* What are your options if the desired behaviour is currently discouraged by negative feedback?

In modifying the payoffs, you have to be creative. Behavioural Modification provides a manageable focus and a framework for analysis; you, as manager, must provide the solution.

Let us consider the problem of Arnold and his 'late reporting'. Firstly, add a negative consequence to Arnold's current behaviour. State explicitly that you need the report by 3.30 on Friday (so that you can prepare your weekly schedule update) – and, if this does not happen, summon Arnold at four o'clock to demand the report before he leaves for the weekend. This will probably ruin his 'hour before the weekend' and he will wish to avoid it in future. Secondly, add a positive consequence to good behaviour. If Arnold does get the report in by 3.30 make a habit of responding to it on Monday morning. If there is an issue raised, help Arnold to address it. If there is a schedule change, talk it over – but make it clear (*say it*) that you are only able to do this because you *had time on Friday* to read his report. Thus Arnold learns that he will receive help and support IF he gets the report in on time.

Stage 6: review
Stage 6 is necessary because such plans do not always work. You must continue to monitor the problem and after a trial period, review your progress. If the plan is working, continue; if the plan has failed, devise a new one; if the plan has worked, look for a new problem to solve.

> *To Practise 9.5:* The only way to practise this technique is to apply the analysis to various problems. Consider your team and identify a problem or a potential improvement. *Write down* the outcome of stages 1, 4 and 5.

9.4 Where to Seek Solutions

The range of problems is so large, that it is impossible to offer more than generalities as advice. Each person is different, each situation is different, so each solution must be carefully crafted. This being said, here are a few ideas.

Be flexible with regards to personal problems. No parent is immune to the 'joys' of a new-born baby, no one is unaffected by bereavement. When circumstances and the human factor impinge upon your ordered plans, adapt; since you cannot change it, work with it. For instance if you sanction a day's 'sick-leave', you might save a week's worry and distraction. Focus upon the problem (say, schedule slippage) and deal with that in the existing situation.

Look for aspects of motivation – any problem which stems from lack of commitment or interest can only successfully be addressed by providing motivation, and any of the motivators described earlier can be applied.

On a larger scale, look carefully at the 'systems' which exist in your team, at those work practices which you and they follow through habit. Some of these can work against you. For instance, the way you hold team meetings may suppress contributions (at 4 o'clock on a Friday, say); the way you reward the exceptional may demotivate those responsible for the mundane.

Take a long-term view. Constant pressure will eventually destroy your team. If you acknowledge that a relaxed yet engaged workforce is (say) 10% more efficient than one which is over-stressed and fretful, then you should realize that this amounts to a half-day per week. So why not devote a half-day to: peer group teaching, brainstorming on enhanced efficiency, visits to customers (internal and external), guest lectures on work tools, or all four on a four-week cycle. You lose nothing if you gain a skilled, committed, and enthusiastic team.

Finally, look carefully at how you behave and whether the current situation is due to your own behaviour. You might be the problem, and the solution.

9.5 A Little Practice

We are going to look at three problems and you are going to try to solve them before reading the suggested solution. These solutions are given to illustrate the principles of the above system – they are unlikely to be the best possible solutions, only you can create those. The problems are drawn from a combination of sources, stories and exercises; so any resemblance between these situations and any you know is purely due to luck.

LAYOUT LAY-ABOUT
As with most management, the problems you encounter will be solved by a little common sense – the difficulty is in recognizing that a problem exists and in thinking it through. Often merely describing a problem will lead to a solution.

140   Starting to Manage

You are not the manager in this case, you are a co-worker in a team which designs microchips. Clive is a 'layout' engineer; this means he is responsible for translating a circuit diagram into a corresponding drawing of intersecting coloured rectangles on a computer screen. While this task does require some knowledge of microelectronics, it is primarily a problem of spatial relations: fitting shapes into gaps. Clive works on several different projects at the same time since the design task alternates between the layout and circuit design phases. There are several layout designers in the team – Clive's work causes the most problems.

Clive is in his early forties and previously worked as an architectural draughtsman where he sometimes supervised junior assistants when the manager was absent. He is well qualified for his current post but, despite his seniority in age, Clive is less well paid than most. According to rumour, he has money problems connected with an old gambling debt. The group manager seems uninterested in Clive's performance and does not involve Clive in any of the design reviews.

Clive's work is of poor quality: the drawings are too spread out (size costs money), they contain errors, they take longer than expected. He is sometimes absent for no given reason, normally leaves early, and takes long lunch breaks. Of all the circuit design engineers, Clive works best for Cecil who tends to explain the circuit's function in detail.

> *To Practise 9.6:* From this information, decide what is relevant and what is not. If you *were* the manager of this group, what actions would you now take?

There are no obvious labels in this description but a lot of the information which could be quantified. You might discretely start keeping track of Clive's periods of absence – you might record the number of drawing errors (particularly if the computer can produce these statistics). These should be tracked to discover the extent of the problem and to give you specific points to raise when you talk to Clive.

The information about Clive's finances is irrelevant since it is beyond the scope of the work relationship.

You need to seek positive payoffs for 'good' behaviour. There are two very significant points in the above history: Clive used to hold a position of greater responsibility, and he responds well to explanations on the background of his assignments. This gives you two possible approaches in devising positive payoffs for good behaviour. The former suggests that Clive should be delegated authority in areas where he can use his training and experience (e.g. coaching new recruits). His poor work is not due to lack of skill and he might be persuaded to display this. The second point suggests that Clive would respond well to being included in the design reviews. There, any contributions he makes will (with your help) earn him recognition and greater involvement. If you can give Clive a feeling of ownership in the designs, he might take greater care.

You also need to find negative payoffs for bad behaviour. Pick one at most. The time-keeping problem is really symptomatic of demotivation so that will probably disappear if the above works. The design errors are detrimental to the whole team – so attack this behaviour. Perhaps, you might introduce a quality programme for the whole team (with displayed, tracked figures) so that peer pressure is applied. Indeed, you might delegate to Clive the job of automating the gathering of such statistics.

> *To Practise 9.7:* But you are not the manager of this group, you are a circuit designer and you have to work with Clive. How are you going to improve the quality of the work Clive does for you?

The same analysis holds – but you have no authority to make sweeping changes or to confront Clive over his short-comings. You should therefore concentrate upon how you interact with Clive, and follow the lead which Cecil has given. When you hand over circuit designs for Clive to lay out, spend a little time talking with him about the circuit. If possible, go over points of the design (especially design options) which will depend upon his work or about which he might have some suggestions. Ask for a firm time by when it will be completed and set aside time then to review the work *with* Clive so that any problems/errors can be discovered and addressed together. If this policy works, tell your colleagues how helpful Clive has been so that his efforts receive recognition and they too learn how to let Clive enjoy his work.

PLAYING WITH FIRE
This is an often used 'person problem' for which the solution has evolved over the years to reflect different philosophies on people management. Personnel officers have argued at length over this one and so there is definitely no 'right' answer. You have to choose.

You are a manager of a team which works in a chemical manufacturing facility. Due to the explosive nature of the materials, there is a strict policy against bringing matches or lighters into the work area. There are large signs over all entrances to warn workers. The stated policy is that offenders will be automatically sacked.

142 Starting to Manage

Debra (Clive's younger sister) does not smoke. But one evening she lights a barbecue at home and puts the matches in the back pocket of her trousers. The next day she goes to work and forgets about the matches until five minutes after she has entered the restricted area. Debra immediately goes to the nearest exit and hands the matches to the security guard – who reports this fact to you.

For your information, risk analysis suggests that an explosion in this area during working hours would result in about twenty fatalities.

> *To Practise 9.8:* You are the manager, what do you do about Debra?

The simple (and much favoured) solution is to sack Debra on the spot; company policy is clearly stated, a severe punishment is desirable since it will act as a deterrent, leniency would make a mockery of the rules and lead to lax (and therefore dangerous) behaviour in the rest of the workforce. Debra should be history.

The alternative solution is to let Debra off. This is justified by the mitigating circumstances: 1) she does not usually carry matches and so was less likely to check, 2) she reported the infringement herself, 3) if she had kept quiet (or simply gone to the toilet), no one would have known – so if you punish her, you are punishing her honesty. Debra would be victim.

The strongest argument in favour of the first solution is that, to be effective, a deterrent has to deter and so it must be both severe and seen to be used. However, there remains the question of degree. In years gone by, the local tyrant might have had Debra flogged to death with a cord of rusty nails and her body strung over the entrance until all the flesh fell off. This would certainly be a deterrent. However, the current labour laws preclude such an effective solution. If you feel that this punishment is a little too severe, then you might like to justify why a good sacking is the most suitable level of punishment. There are many infringements Debra could have committed – for which sacking would be the only option. Is this necessarily one of them? Could you not react in a manner which both reinforces the deterrent and achieves some other positive benefit?

> *To Practise 9.9: Write down* any behaviour which you wish to encourage or discourage in relation to matches and explosives.

A third solution requires a bit of careful thought about behaviour. In this solution you recognize the company policy for what it is: a simple (crude) behavioural modifier with a secondary advantage in that it allows the company to fire any offender without falling foul of the employment legislation. As an enlightened manager, you might recognize that the plan (to keep matches away from the explosives) has failed and that this is actually your main problem. Debra is a not the issue.

While you clearly want to keep matches out of the facility, you do not want people who fall through the system (like Debra) to keep quiet about matches in the explosives area simply to keep their jobs. Whatever system you have in place must cater for real situations rather than assuming the ideal. Once she had made the mistake and realized it, Debra reacted with the best possible behaviour – and you do not want to discourage that.

Since Debra did break the (sacred) rule, she needs to be punished. She probably expects it, so there is no reason to disappoint her; without a punishment, your authority is compromised if you later have to deal with a malicious offender. If you select something which is visible to the rest of the workforce, then the deterrent remains in place. If you couple that with a new twist to the 'no-matches-rule' then you also address the problem of improving safety. Perhaps Debra should (in her own time) prepare an event (a graphic poster, a presentation, a stunt) to reinforce the safety message. Perhaps she should attend a course on first-aid for burn victims which she then teaches to the rest of the staff during her free day. You choose. But determine your objective first; do not merely react.

HEALING THE STOCK

This example is to illustrate that a little creativity goes a long way. You are in charge of supplies at a large city hospital. The stock room is open to all nurses and porters (using a security card) and they are asked to fill out a record for any stock they take so that the correct cost centre can be billed and the stocks replenished. However, most stock leaves unrecorded since staff dislike spending time filling out forms ('when they could be helping patients'). Theft is not the problem. So far, the administration has tried lectures, threats, and regular announcements of financial loss; but all to no avail.

> *To Practise 9.10:* Devise a system to solve this problem. Your thoughts should focus on providing a positive pay-off for the desired behaviour.

Simply stated, you want the nurses and porters to fill out the forms. One solution is to reduce losses by employing a clerk to oversee the stock room and to provide material only in return for a correctly filled form. Thus the reward for filling in a form is the goods themselves. This would probably work but it might be slow, there may be queues, it costs a 24-hour salary and it adds bureaucracy rather than team spirit.

An alternative solution is as follows. The hospital announces that 1% of the value of all stock-withdrawals correctly recorded will be donated to a third-world medical charity. 1% is small, the hospital can afford that in preference to the current losses, but it does not actually produce impressive sounding donations. So the 'results' are posted in terms of practical aid given in the third world where a little money goes a long way. So the nurses of Ward 10 paid for ten sight-saving cataract operations, the porters together managed to provide ten children with clean drinking water for ten months, and the theatre nurses managed to send ten days' supply of food to a leper colony. A little creativity, a few posters, regular changes in focus for the funds, and no dedicated hospital worker would fail to fill out a form which saves a starving child.

Focus upon the behaviour you want, find a reward they want, marry the two and everybody wins.

9.6 A Manager of the People

To practise this focus upon people, start by recalling exactly what they mean to you. If you were a craftsman, you would take care of your work tools; if you were a mountain climber, you would always check your ropes; if you were in the armed forces, you would treat your weapon with respect. The inanimate tools of skill, safety and survival receive your attention as a matter of simple common sense – so too should your team. They are also the tools of your trade and they need maintenance, careful handling and regular inspection to enable them to work at full performance.

To play *Watch your Team* (a new game for this chapter) draw a grid with the five motivators along one axis and the names of each team member along the other. In each intersecting square, write what you believe to be the most significant factor which currently provides that motivator to that person. For each person, decide which square was hardest to fill in and determine how to modify that person's work/responsibility to add a new factor to that square. If this analysis reveals a 'person problem' – deal with it.

Summary of People

Positive Motivators

Achievement	(choose their targets)
Recognition	(praise the good - give clear guidance for improving the bad)
The Work	(work to make it interesting)
Advancement	(provided in small steps)
Responsibility	(to the maximum)

To Modify Behaviour

Specify	(without labels)
Monitor	(to see if real, to mark the start)
Discuss	(communicate your concern)
Analyse	(when all else fails, think about it)
Modify Payoffs	(the 'carrot and stick' approach)
Review	(no management process is complete without it)

Chapter: 10
Planning a Project

The best laid schemes o' mice an' men, gang aft a-gley
(Robert Burns)

When you and your team are given a task, it has to be organized. As the manager, you have to interpret the instructions and turn them into a plan of action which will lead to the completion of the task. To muddle through this, all you need to do is to give it exclusively to one good worker and wait for the results. If your boss asks for an update, always be confidently positive and make vague references to 'slight slippages' balanced by strong assertions of 'progressing well'; avoid any answers that include numbers or dates – these come back to haunt you. If you are lucky, the project will be so delayed that it will no longer be needed; otherwise you should invest some time in the necessary documentation: your personal résumé or curriculum vitae.

Of course, to be a *great* manager you need a slightly different approach. To allow your team to take an active role in the work they do from one day to the next, you must devise and communicate a structure for each project which embodies not only the work itself but also a *reasonable* set of expectations. Thus the team each have a full picture of where their own work fits into the work of the whole team, and a goal or guideline by which to measure personal performance. As a manager you have to provide a structure which is demanding (to stretch them), exciting (to motivate them) and attainable (to build confidence them). You have to do all this AND get it right. This chapter provides the basics of project planning, with emphasis on how to avoid the more common pitfalls.

10.1 Project Management

To manage a project you have to:

- Understand what is required
- Devise a plan of activities by which this can be achieved
- Match these activities to actual people
- Produce a schedule by which progress can be monitored
- Review progress against the schedule and in light of new information
- Revise the plan as necessary
- Review the management of the project on completion

And this is the simple list dealing only with your own team. Further complications arise because your project is part of a larger project and other teams, people, customers, events, catastrophes, all impact upon your ordered plans.

Most management of a project depends almost entirely upon the planning and the procedures established *at the beginning* of the project. Thus the success of a project will depend critically upon the effort, care and skill you apply to its initial planning. As your responsibility for organization increases, this is the skill by which you will ultimately be judged.

> *To Practise 10.1:* To start with, you need to establish your current projects: these are all the tasks for which you and your team are responsible. If you cannot write these down, you may have found a problem. Choose one project and consider the bullet points above.

10.2 The Specification

Before describing the role and creation of a specification, we need to introduce and explain a fairly technical term: a *numbty* is a person whose brain is totally numb. In this context, numb means 'deprived of feeling or the power of unassisted activity'; in general, a numbty needs the stimulation of an electric cattle prod even to get to the right office in the morning. Communication with numbties is severely hampered by the fact that although they think they know what they mean (which they do not), they seldom actually say it, and they never write it down. And the main employment of numbties world-wide is in the creation of project specifications. As a manager, you must know this – and protect your team accordingly.

A specification is the definition of your project: a statement of the problem, not the solution. When you first hear of a project, it is seldom in writing, it is commonly someone's 'bright idea'. If you are lucky, it will be the result of much thought and perhaps preliminary study; normally, however, it comes from a numbty. In this case the specification contains errors, ambiguities, misunderstandings and enough rope to hang you and your entire team. Thus before you embark upon the the next six months of activity working on the wrong project, you must put huge amounts of effort into understanding and clarifying the specification. Without spending time on settling the specification, you might as well not start the project at all.

> When the tunnel under the English Channel was built, the French started at one end and the British started at the other. What if .... ?
>
> *Yes, exactly 1050 yards!*
>
> *Oui, exactement 1050 metres!*

This is your job. You have to protect your team from poor specifications. You must assume that a numbty was the chief author of every specification you receive and you must read, worry, revise and ensure that everyone concerned with the project (from originator, through the workers, to the end-customer) is working with the same understanding. The outcome of this deliberation should be a *written* definition of what is required, by when; and this must be *agreed* by all involved. There are no short-cuts to this. If you fail to spend the time initially, it will cost you far more later on.

The *agreement* upon a *written* specification has several benefits:
- the clarity will reveal misunderstandings
- the completeness will remove contradictory assumptions
- the rigour of the analysis will expose technical and practical details which numbties normally gloss over through ignorance or fear
- the agreement forces all concerned to actually read and think about the details

The work on the specification can be seen as the first stage of Quality Assurance since you are looking for and countering problems in the very foundation of the project – from this perspective the creation of the specification clearly merits a large investment of time.

From a purely defensive point of view, the agreed specification also affords you protection from numbties who have second thoughts, or new ideas, half-way through the project. Once the project is underway, changes cost time (and money). The existence of a demonstrably-agreed specification enables you to resist or to charge (possibly in terms of extra time) for such changes. Further, people tend to forget what they originally thought; you may need proof that you have been working as instructed.

> *To Practise 10.2:* Thinking about previous projects, where did the discrepancies arise between what was done and what was wanted?

The places to look for errors in a specification are:

- the global context: numbties often focus too narrowly on the work of one team and fail to consider how it fits into the larger picture. Some of the work given to you may actually be undone or duplicated by others. Some of the proposed work may be incompatible with that of others; it might be just plain barmy in the larger context.

- the interfaces: between your team and both its customers and suppliers, there are interfaces. At these points something gets transferred. Exactly what, how and when should be discussed and agreed from the very beginning. Never assume a common understanding, because you will be wrong. All it takes for your habitual understandings to evaporate is the arrival or departure of one person. Define and agree your interfaces and maintain a friendly contact throughout the project.

- time-scales: numbties always underestimate the time involved for work. If there are no time-scales in the specification, you can assume that one will be imposed upon you (which will be impossible). You must add realistic dates. The detail should include a precise understanding of the extent of any intermediate stages of the task, particularly those which have to be delivered.

- external dependencies: your work may depend upon that of others. Make this very clear so that these people too will receive warning of your needs. Highlight the effect that problems with these would have upon your project so that everyone is quite clear about their importance. To be sure, contact these people yourself and ask if they are able to fulfil the assumptions in your specification.

- resources: the numbty tends to ignore resources. The specification should identify the materials, equipment and manpower which are needed for the project. The agreement should include a commitment by your managers to allocate or fund them. You should check that the actual numbers are practical and/or correct. If they are omitted, add them – there are bound to be differences in assumed values.

This seems to make the specification sound like a long document. It should not be. Each of the above could be a simple sub-heading followed by either bullet points or a table – you are not writing a brochure, you are stating the definition of the project in clear, concise and unambiguous glory.

Of course, the specification may change. If circumstances, or simply your knowledge, change then the specification will be out of date. You should not regard it as cast in stone but rather as a display board where everyone involved can see the current, common understanding of the project. If you change the content everyone must know, but do not hesitate to change it as necessary.

> *To Practise 10.3:* Take the project from the first question and consider your understanding of the specification. Try to *write it down* (clearly and concisely) and then show it to the originator.

10.3 Providing Structure

As a manager, you must provide a structure to the work for your team. This serves two functions: 1) it allows you to communicate the project to your team in terms of its components, and 2) it helps you to allocate the actual work which needs to be done.

The work each person has to do is far more detailed, and focused on minutiae, than your complete overview of the project. To maintain their interest (and motivation), you must communicate how that work fits into the whole project. The explicit structure of the project allows them to see where their individual work contributes to the whole. Thus, they will enjoy common ownership and purpose. Without an understanding of this structure, their work is a series of unrelated tasks providing little sense of achievement and no feeling of advancement.

To decide what actually has to be done, you have to break the project down into manageable chunks and then produce a plan by which these chunks can be recombined over time into the original project.

Work Breakdown Structure

Once you have a clear understanding of the project, and eliminated the vagaries of the numbties, you then describe it as a set of simpler separate *activities*. If any of these are still too complex for you to organize easily, you break them down also into another level of simpler descriptions, and so on until you can manage everything. Thus, your one complex project is organized as a set of simple tasks which together achieve the desired result.

The reasoning behind this is that the human brain (even yours) can only take in and process so much information at one time. To get a real grasp of the project, you have to think about it in large pieces rather than try to process the complexity of its details all at once. Thus each level of the project can be understood as the amalgamation of a few simply described smaller units.

Suppose you have a party to arrange. First of all you want to make sure that you remember everything; so you make a list of all the things you have to do. The list consists of the main categories like invitations, food, venue, etc because these, you know, have to be done. You do not start by deciding between salted and dry-roasted peanuts, you start with the large bold brushstrokes. The *project* is split into a list of (say) six main *activities*, and then you consider each activity separately and make lists for each of these.

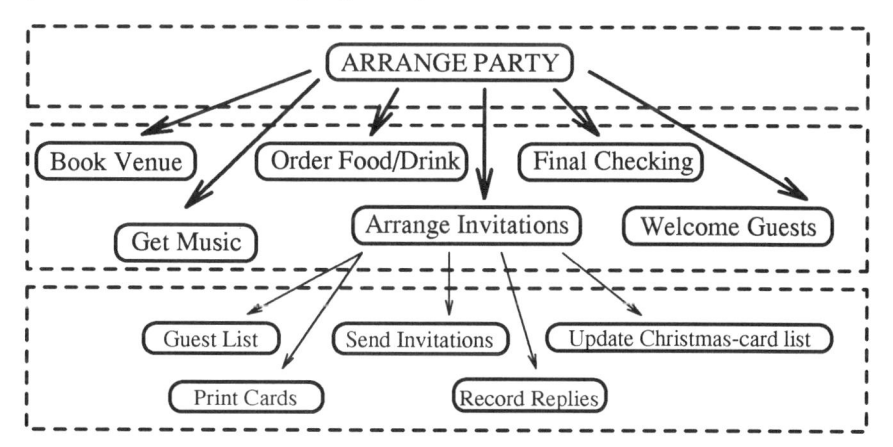

```
                    ARRANGE PARTY
        /        /        |        \
   Book Venue  Order Food/Drink  Final Checking
        Get Music   Arrange Invitations   Welcome Guests
                    /        |        \
            Guest List   Send Invitations   Update Christmas-card list
               Print Cards        Record Replies
```

In planning any project, you follow the same simple steps: big items become lists of smaller ones. People call this producing a *work breakdown structure* to make it sound formal and impressive. At each stage, your common sense will tell you what is too complicated to manage, and so it becomes another list. Without following this formal approach you are unlikely to remember all the niggling little details; with this procedure, the details are simply displayed on the final lists.

Commonly, each item can be assigned to one individual and so forms a short-term goal for that person. Its place in the work breakdown structure allows him/her to see where the work fits into, and contributes to, the whole project and so there is a clear sense of personal contribution.

One common fault is to produce too much detail at the initial planning stage. You should stop when you have a sufficient description of the activity to provide a clear instruction for the person who will actually do the work, and to have a reasonable estimate for the total time/effort involved. You need the former to allocate (or delegate) the task; you need the latter to finish the planning.

> *To Practise 10.4:* Take your project and start planning it afresh. Paint the first broad strokes of the work breakdown structure (lists of lists).

Task Allocation and Scheduling

The next stage is a little complicated. You now have to allocate the tasks to different people in the team and, at the same time, order these tasks so that they are performed in a sensible sequence.

Task allocation is not simply a case of handing out the various tasks on your final lists to the people you have available; it is far more subtle (and powerful) than that. As a manager your role as Planner means that you have to look far beyond the single project; indeed any individual project should be seen as merely a single step in your team's development. The allocation of tasks should thus be seen as a means of increasing the skills and experience of your team – when the project is done, the team should have gained.

In simple terms, consider the capability of each person in the team, and allocate tasks of sufficient complexity to match (or slightly more, to stretch). The tasks you allocate are *not* the ones on your final lists, they are adapted to better suit your needs of team development.

> TASKS ARE MOULDED TO FIT PEOPLE

which is far more effective than the other way around. If Arnold is to learn something new, the task may be simplified with responsibility given to another to guide and check the work; if Brenda is to develop, sufficient tasks are combined so that her responsibility increases beyond that which she has held before; if Colin lacks confidence, the tasks are broken into smaller units which can be completed (and commended) frequently.

Sometimes tasks can be grouped and allocated together. For instance, two tasks which are seemingly independent may benefit from being done together since they use common ideas, information, talents. One person doing them both removes the start-up time for one of them; two people (one on each) can help each other.

The ordering of the tasks is really quite simple, although you may find that sketching a diagram helps you to think it through (and to communicate the result).

For example, if Y cannot be started until X is finished then Y follows X. If Y and Z are totally independent (but both need X to finish first) then they can be done in either order or at the same time. Of course if they are done in parallel they may take just as long in total as if they had been done in sequence, unless you put two people on the job: one for Y and one for Z.

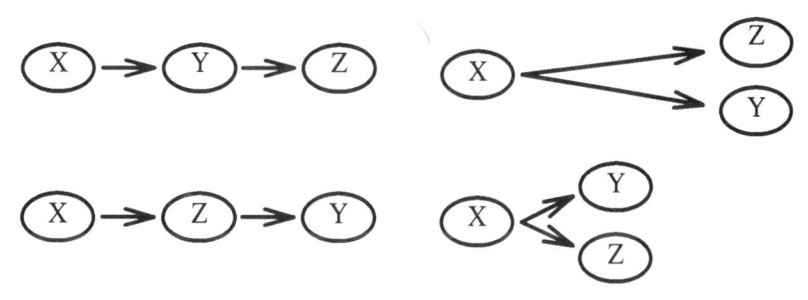

```
X → Y → Z        X ⟶ Z
                   ⟶ Y

X → Z → Y        X → Y
                   → Z
```

The more people you have the more independent tasks can be done together; but in any project there is a limit to the number of tasks which are truly independent and so extra resources will not always lead to faster results.

Getting the details of the schedule exactly right can be a long and painful process, and often it can be futile. The degree to which you can predict the future is limited, so too should be the detail of your planning. You must have the broad outlines by which to monitor progress, and sufficient detail to assign each task when it needs to be started, but beyond that – stop and do something useful instead.

> *To Practise 10.5:* Consider each person in your team (possibly using your notes from the end of chapter 9) and mould the tasks of your project to meet (for each person) *one* development need.

Guesstimation

At the initial planning stage the main objective is to get a *realistic* estimate of the time involved in the project. As manager you must establish this not only to assist higher management with their planning, but also to protect your team from being expected to do the impossible. The most important technique for achieving this is known as: *guesstimation*.

Guesstimating schedules is notoriously difficult but it is helped by two approaches:

- make your guesstimates of the simple tasks at the bottom of the work breakdown structure and look for the longest path through the sequence diagram
- use the experience from previous projects to improve your guesstimating skills

The corollary to this is that you should keep records in an easily accessible form of all projects as you do them. Part of your final project review should be to update your personal data base of how long various activities take. This phase is vital to your success as a manager.

Some people find guesstimating a difficult concept in that if you have no experience of an activity, how can you make a worthwhile estimate? Let us consider such a problem: how long would it take you to walk all the way to the top of the Eiffel Tower or the Statue of Liberty? Presuming you have never actually tried this (most people use the elevator), you really have very little to go on. Indeed if you have actually seen one (and only one) of these structures, think about the other. Your job depends on this, so think carefully. One idea is to start with the number of steps – guess that if you can. Notice, you do not have to be right, merely reasonable. Next, consider the sort of pace you could maintain while climbing a flight of steps for a long time. Now imagine yourself at the base of a flight of steps you do know, and estimate a) how many steps there are, and b) how long it takes you to climb them (at that steady pace). To complete, apply a little mathematics.

Now examine how confident you are with this estimate. If you won a free flight to Paris or New York and tried it, you would probably (need your head examined) be mildly surprised if you climbed to the top in less than half the estimated time and if it took you more than double you would be mildly annoyed. If it took you less than a tenth the time, or ten times as long, you would be extremely surprised/annoyed. In fact, you do not currently believe that that would happen (no really, do you?). The point is that from very little experience of the given problem, you can actually come up with a working estimate – and one which is far better than no estimate at all when it comes to deriving a schedule. Guesstimating does take a little practice, but it is a very useful skill to develop.

> *To Practise 10.6:* How long would it take you to write a 100-word explanation of guesstimation for your team? Test your answer.

Practical Problems

There are several practical problems in guesstimation. To begin with, you are simply too optimistic. It is human nature at the beginning of a new project to ignore the difficulties and assume best case scenarios – in producing your estimates (and using those of others) you must inject a little realism. In practice, you should also build in a little slack to allow yourself some tolerance against mistakes. This is known as *defensive scheduling*. Also, if you deliver ahead of the agreed schedule, you will be loved.

You will be under pressure from senior management to deliver quickly, especially if the project is being sold competitively. Resist the temptation to rely upon speed as the only selling point. You might, for instance, suggest the criteria of fewer errors, history of adherence to initial schedules, and/or previous customer satisfaction: 'This is how long it takes, so how can you trust the other quotes?'.

When forming guesstimates of task duration, you also have to consider the people allocated to that task. Your aim is to produce the schedule not for the ideal team, but rather for your existing team. Thus you must consider the pace at which individuals work, their familiarity with the tasks, the time needed to learn new skills and even the impact that one person learning a new skill will have on anyone else who offers to help.

Generally, guesstimates tend to ignore time spent upon other activities. Your team has many tasks associated with managing the project (rather than doing it), with being part of the company, with simply 'ticking over'. These will affect the elapsed time of any project – and you must take them into account when planning the schedules. Commonly missed is the fact that people have holidays. Sometimes people are even ill; you should not allow a major-project schedule to be endangered by one broken leg.

10.4 Establishing Controls

When the planning phase is over (and agreed), the 'doing' phase begins. Once it is in motion, a project acquires a direction and momentum which is totally independent of anything you predicted. If you come to terms with that from the start, you can then enjoy the roller-coaster which follows. To gain some hope, however, you need to establish at the start (within the plan) the means to monitor and influence the project's progress.

There are two key elements to the control of a project

- milestones (clear, unambiguous targets of what, by when)
- established means of communication

For you, the milestones are a mechanism to monitor progress; for your team, they are short-term goals which are far more tangible than the foggy, distant completion of the entire project. The milestones maintain the momentum and encourage effort. They allow the team to judge their own progress and to celebrate achievement throughout the project rather than just at its end.

The simplest way to construct milestones is to take the timing information from the work breakdown structure and sequence diagram. When you have guesstimated how long each sub-task will take and have strung them together, you can identify by when each of these tasks will actually be completed. This is simple and effective; however, it lacks creativity.

A second method is to construct more significant milestones. These can be found by identifying stages in the development of a project which are recognizable as steps towards the final product. Sometimes these are simply the higher levels of your structure; for instance, the completion of a market-evaluation phase. Sometimes, they cut across many parallel activities; for instance, a prototype of the eventual product or a mock-up of the new brochure format.

If you are running activities in parallel, this type of milestone is particularly useful since it provides a means of pulling together the people on disparate activities so that:

- they all have a shared goal (the common milestone)
- their responsibility to (and dependence upon) each other is emphasized
- each can provide a new (but informed) viewpoint on the others' work
- the problems to do with combining the different activities are highlighted and discussed early in the implementation phase

- you have something tangible which senior management (and numbties) can recognize as progress
- you have something tangible which your team can celebrate and which constitutes a short-term goal in a possibly long-term project
- it provides an excellent opportunity for review and for quality checking

Of course, there are milestones and there are mill-stones. You will have to be sensitive to any belief that working for some specific milestone is hindering rather than helping the work forward. If this arises then either you have chosen the wrong milestone, or you have failed to communicate how it fits into the broader structure.

> *To Practise 10.7: Write down* your project's milestones. What happens if these are delayed? When would you know? When would you take action? Usually when your team misses a milestone, is it because 1) your estimates are wrong, 2) their motivation is low, or 3) some other reason?

Communication is your everything. To monitor progress, to receive early warning of danger, to promote cooperation, to motivate through team involvement, all of these rely upon communication. At the initial stages of a project (when little is happening beyond the planning), it is easy to keep track of events by simply walking about and having a few (managed) conversations. Often this will lull you into a false sense of security and overconfidence. However, if things start to go wrong, the first thing that will slip are these leisured chats (as you become too busy), yet the last thing you should lose is communication. In a crisis, communication is vital. Thus you need to establish from the beginning the mechanisms by which communication continues automatically.

Regular reports are useful – if you clearly define what information is needed and if you teach your team how to provide it in a rapidly accessible form (see chapter 5). Often these reports merely say 'progressing according to schedule'. These you send back, for while the message is desired the evidence is missing; you must insist that your team monitor their own progress with concrete, tangible, measurements and if this is done, the figures should be included in the report. However, the real value of this practice comes when progress is not according to schedule – then your communication system is worth all the effort you invested in its planning.

Another useful practice is to hold regular 'progress reviews' where people can discuss and share their experiences. Especially if your project involves something totally new (about which all are learning) then the team review is the only way to pool all the practical experience and so help the team to produce new ideas (see chapter 3). Let us say that again. If your project involves walking 'into the unknown' then you will need all the help that your team can give you. You will need to manage carefully the first few furtive steps by encouraging frequent reviews and discussion. Since you are not sure (through collective inexperience) where you are going, you will need to take smaller steps and larger reviews.

> *To Practise 10.8:* Would your channels of communication survive in a crisis?

10.5 The Artistry in Planning

At the planning stage, you can deal with far more than the mere project at hand. You can shape the overall strengths of your team by using the division and type of activities you assign. The following are a few points to consider when planning a project.

Who know best?
Ask your team. They too must be involved in the planning of projects, especially in the lower levels of the work breakdown structure. Not only will they provide information and ideas, but also they will feel ownership in the final plan.

This does not mean that your projects should be planned by committee – rather that you, as manager, plan the project based upon all the available experience and creative ideas. As an initial approach, you could attempt the first level(s) of the work breakdown structure to help you communicate the project to the team and then ask for comments. Then, using these, the final levels could be refined by the people to whom the tasks will be allocated. However, since the specification is so vital, *all* the team should vet the penultimate draft.

Dangers in review
There are two pitfalls to avoid in project reviews:

- they can be too frequent
- they can be too drastic

The constant trickle of new information can lead to a vicious cycle of planning and revising which shakes the team's confidence in any particular version of the plan and which destroys the very stability which the structure was designed to provide. You must decide the balance. Pick a point on the horizon and walk confidently towards it. Decide objectively, and explain beforehand, when the review will take place and make this a scheduled milestone in itself.

Even though the situation may have changed since the last review, it is important to recognize the work which has been accomplished during the interim. Firstly, you do not want to abandon it since the team will be demotivated, feeling that they have achieved nothing. Secondly, this work itself is part of the new situation: it has been done, it should provide a foundation for the next step or at least the basis of a lesson well learnt. Always try to build upon the existing achievements of your team.

Testing and Quality
No plan is complete without explicit provision for testing and quality. As an enlightened manager (having read chapter 7) you will know that this should be part of each individual phase of the project. This means that no activity is completed until it has passed the (objectively) defined criteria which establish its quality, and these are best defined (objectively) at the beginning as part of the planning.

When devising the schedule, therefore, you must include allocated time for this part of each activity. Thus your question is not only, 'How long will it take?', but also, 'How long will the testing take?'. By asking both questions together you raise the issue of, 'How do we know we have done it right?' at the very beginning and so the testing is more likely to be done in parallel with the implementation. You establish this philosophy for your team by including testing as a justified (required) cost.

For larger projects, it might also be wise to make 'implementation of test strategy' an additional, resourced activity. In this way, some time will be devoted to planning testing across the whole project, so covering a scope that individual activities might miss. Of course, this must not degenerate into a straight fight between the testers and the do-ers; rather the testers should be providing a service for the whole team by integrating and taking part in the individual activities' test strategies. For instance, the testers might decide that a customer trial is needed. They might then arrange an event where selected customers (internal and/or external) are asked to comment upon a prototype or mock-up of the final service or product. You will need to decide initially if this scale of activity is needed and if it is, you must allocate time and resources in the schedule from the beginning. Put another way, if this happens as merely an after-thought, it will play havoc with your schedule and show that your planning was flawed.

Fitness for purpose

Another reason for stating the testing criteria at the beginning is that you can avoid futile quests for perfection. If you have motivated your team well, they will take pride in their work and want to do the best job possible. Often this means polishing their work until it shines; often this wastes time. If it is clear at the onset exactly what is needed, then they are more likely to stop when that has been achieved. You need to avoid generalities and to stipulate boundaries; not easy, but essential.

The same is also true when choosing the tools or building-blocks of your project. While it might be nice to have the most modern version of equipment, or to develop a newer version to match your needs, often there is an old/existing version which will serve almost as well (sufficient for the purpose), and the difference is not worth the time you would need to invest in obtaining or developing the new one. Use what is available whenever possible unless the *difference* is worth the time, money and initial teething pains.

A related idea is that you should discourage too much effort on aspects of the project which are idiosyncratic. In the specification phase, you might try to eliminate these through negotiation with the customer; in the implementation phase you might leave these parts until last. The reason for this advice is that a *general* piece of work can be tailored to many specific instances; thus, if the work is kept in a general form, you will be able to rapidly re-use it for other projects. On the other hand, if you produce something which is cut to fit exactly one specific case, you may have to repeat the work entirely even though the next project is fairly similar. At the planning phase, a manager should bear in mind the future and the long-term development of the team as well as the requirements of the current project.

Enable experimentation

If you need to rely upon the creativity of your team you will need to enable innovation. The problem with innovation is that things go wrong; in fact, they normally do. If you want innovation, therefore, you must allow for errors not only in terms of the time you allocate to 'exploration', but also by your reaction to failure. The optimal situation is that there is an existing fall back position (if nothing else we can write the tables by hand within five days) and so you can allow experiments to run until the deadline dictates that the fall-back strategy has to be used.

Even the failure, though, can (should) be seen as useful. Any experiment provides knowledge, since if you had known the answer before, you would not have needed to try it out. This new knowledge is beneficial to the long-term objectives of the team since if the experiment is futile it will not be tried again and so time will be saved; if it is partially successful it may suggest a solution in different circumstances. You, as manager, must ensure that these failures are milked for all the information they have generated and that this information is retained by the team for its future.

Fighting for time

As a manager, you have to regulate the pressure and work load which is imposed upon your team; you must protect them from the unreasonable demands of the rest of the company. Once you have arrived at what you consider to be a realistic schedule, fight for it. Never let the outside world deflect you from what you know to be practical. If they impose a deadline upon you which is impossible, *clearly* state this and give your reasons. You will need to give some room for compromise, however, since a flat **NO** will be seen as obstructive. Since you want to help the company, you should look for alternative positions. For instance:

You could offer a prototype service or product at an earlier date. This might, in some cases, be sufficient for the customer to start the next stage of his/her own project on the understanding that your project would be completed at a later date and the final version would then replace the prototype.

The complexity of the product, or the number of units, could be reduced. This might, in some cases, be sufficient for the customer's immediate needs. Future enhancements or more units would then be the subject of a subsequent negotiation which, you feel, would be likely to succeed since you will have already demonstrated your ability to deliver on time.

You could produce an alternative schedule showing how the deadline might be met with additional (specified) resources or by rescheduling other projects. Thus, you provide a clear picture of the situation and a possible solution; it is then up to your manager to decide how to proceed.

Planning for error

The most common error in planning is to assume that there will be no errors. In effect, the schedule is derived on the basis of 'if nothing goes wrong, this will take ...'. Of course, recognizing that errors *will* occur is the reason for implementing a monitoring strategy on the project. Thus, when the inevitable does happen, you can react and adapt the plan to compensate. However, by carefully considering errors in advance you can make changes to the original plan to enhance its tolerance. Quite simply, your planning should include time where you stand back from the design and ask, *'What can go wrong?'*. This is an excellent way of asking your team for their analysis of your plan.

You can try to predict where the errors will occur. By examining the list of activities, you can usually pinpoint some activities which are risky (for instance, those involving new equipment) and others which are quite secure (for instance, those which your team has done often before). The risky areas might then be given a less stringent time-scale – actually planning time for mistakes. Another possibility is to apply a different strategy, or more resources, to such activities to minimize the disruption. For instance, you could include training or consultancy for new equipment, or you might parallel the work with the foundation of a fall-back position.

Another approach is to play *'what if ...'* games. These are particularly useful when catering for problems resulting from external events. So if you are depending upon a delivery of material or information by an agreed date, ask yourself (or your team), 'what will happen if this is a week late?'. The answers you get from such games may either drive you to an early grave or allow you to undertake defensive planning. For instance, you could identify activities which need not be tackled then, but which could be if the manpower were available (perhaps due to late delivery of material for their planned work); alternatively you could delegate to someone the task of liaising with the supplier to obtain early warning about the potential problem.

Double accounting

The final output of your deliberations is really two plans: one for publication to higher management (possibly the first level of decomposition plus the major milestones) and one for the team (with all the gory detail) giving each person his/her allotted tasks. Both of these require effort in their communication; aim always for the simplest possible display.

Of course, you might also wish to produce different versions of your schedules: one which you believe, and one which adds a larger margin of error so that you will either deliver despite difficulty or appear a hero for delivering early. This is something you must decide in the light of your relationship with your own managers.

Post-mortem

At the end of any project, you should allocate time to reviewing the lessons of, and information about, both the work itself and the management of that work: an open meeting, with open discussion, with the whole team and all customers and suppliers. If you think that this might be thought a waste of time by your own manager, think of the effect it will have on future communications with your customers and suppliers.

> *To Practise 10.9:* Consider how your current project planning caters for each of the headings in this section.

10.6 Planning for the Future

With all these considerations in merely the 'planning' stage of a project, it is perhaps surprising that projects get done at all. In fact projects do get done, but seldom in the predicted manner and often as much by brute force as by careful planning. The point, however, is that the latter method is non-optimal. Customers feel let down by late delivery, staff are demotivated by constant pressure towards impossible goals, corners get cut which harms your reputation, and each project has to overcome the same problems as the last.

With planning, projects can run on time and interact effectively with both customers and suppliers. Everyone involved understands what is wanted and emerging problems are seen (and dealt with) long before they cause damage. If you want your projects to run this way – then you must invest the necessary time in planning.

This game is called *'Watch the Projects'*. You need to devise a personal check-list on how to plan a project. Based upon this chapter and the planning you have done already, write out a list of actions (criteria) you have to take (consider) for each project plan. Whenever a project goes badly wrong, update this list with an item to counter that problem in the future. At the end of each project (after the post-mortem) choose which entry was the most significant to that project and move it to the top of the list. Finally, get other managers to talk about their projects and problems; this will give you practice in managing conversations, and the experience of other people's mistakes.

Summary of Project Planning

Refine ('worry') the specification   - written
                                     - agreed

Seek errors in   - global context
                 - interfaces
                 - time-scales
                 - external dependencies
                 - resources and numbers

Structure to   - construct plan
               - capture plan
               - communicate plan

Work Breakdown Structure (lists of lists)
Mould tasks to teams
String tasks together
Guesstimate schedules

Control   - milestones
          - establish communicaton

Plan includes   - asking the team
                - testing for quality
                - fitness for purpose
                - error prediction
                - alternative schedules

Chapter: 11
A Great Manager

Few people think more than two or three times a year; I have made an international reputation for myself by thinking once or twice a week
(George Bernard Shaw)

Now that we have looked at the *essential* skills, it is worth pausing in this chapter (before passing the book to a colleague) to reflect a little further on what makes a *great* manager. The following are a variety of disparate thoughts and personal views; as always, you should decide for yourself.

11.1 The Main Theme

In case it is not absurdly obvious by now, this book has two main messages:
- you have the power to shape your own team and work environment
- all you need to do is to use your own common sense

Whenever you have something to do, consider not only the task but first of all the process. Thus if there is a meeting to decide the marketing slogan for the new product, you should initially ignore anything to do with marketing slogans and decide: 1) how should the meeting be held, 2) who can usefully contribute, 3) how will ideas be best generated, 4) what criteria are involved in the decision, 5) is there a better way of achieving the same end, 6) etc. If you resolve these points first, all will be achieved far more smoothly. Many of these decisions do not have a single 'right' answer, the point is that they need to have 'an' answer so that the task is accomplished efficiently. It is the posing of the questions in the first place which will mark you out as a really *great* manager – the solutions are available to you through common sense.

Once the questions are posed, you can be creative. For instance, 'is there a better way of producing a new slogan?' could be answered by a quick internal competition within the company (answers on a postcard by tomorrow at noon) asking everybody in the company to contribute an idea first. This takes three minutes and a secretary to organize, it provides a quick buzz of excitement throughout the whole company, it refocuses everyone's mind on the new product and so celebrates its success, all staff feel some ownership of the project, and you start the meeting with several ideas either from which to select a winner or to use as triggers for further brainstorming. Thus with a simple -- pause -- from the helter-skelter of getting the next job done, and a moment's reflection, you can expedite the task and build team spirit throughout the entire company.

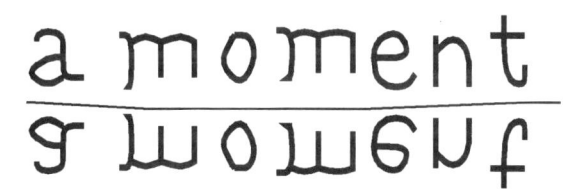

$$\frac{a\ moment}{a\ moment}$$

To refine this ability, you need to ask questions, observe others, and think through solutions. Watching others at work is the simplest teacher of all since the experience of others is all around you, and you gain from both their experience and the knowledge you derive concerning the strengths of the troupe. If you are watching for technique, and trying to understand the reasoning behind it, you learn a great deal about the people concerned.

It is the questioning which is the hardest part to adopt. This must become simple habit. For reactive opportunities (ones given to you) this comes more easily since when the situation or task is presented to you for the first time, the novelty can be used to prompt you to pause and reflect. Thereafter, you can regularize your questioning by designating a review when you again pause to reflect, and repeat.

It is in the proactive situations (ones you initiate) where the questioning is harder since it depends upon you raising the question in the first place. To cater for long-term planning, staff development, or everything that you might blunder through without explicitly managing; you need to track such tasks by linking them to regular reviews or other recurrent activity. Thus, staff development is an issue which may come up in the performance reviews you have to conduct; long-term planning could be something you do on the first day of each month.

Once you have identified a question you might seldom ask (and so a problem which might escape your common sense), note it down where you will be reminded of it from time to time – just to be safe. In fact, the questions will often be answered easily because, with them on your mind, you will recognize opportunities and solutions when they appear.

11.2 Starting a Revolution

The idea of starting alone, however, may still be daunting to you; you may not see yourself as a David against the Goliath of other people's (low) expectations. The bad news is that you will meet resistance to change. Your salvation lies in convincing your team (who are most affected) that what you are doing can only do them good, and in convincing everyone else that it can do them no harm. The good news is that others might soon follow you.

There is precedent for this. For instance, when a British firm called Unipart wanted to introduce Japanese methods (Honda's to be precise) into their Oxford plant[†] they sent a small team to Japan to learn what exactly this meant. On their return, the travellers were mocked by their workmates who saw them as management pawns. So they formed their own team and went to work in a corner of the plant where they applied their new knowledge in isolation. Slowly, but surely, their example (and missionary zeal) spread through the factory and changes followed. Now Unipart have opened a new factory and the general manager of the first factory attributes the success to 'releasing talent already on the shop floor'. Of course one can always find case studies to support any management idea, but it does exemplify the potential of a small cell of dedicated zealots – led by you.

One way to overcome some of the resistance within the company is actively to promote the identity and success of your team. There are many simple and seemingly trivial ways to do this. For instance, give them a name. If they have one already, change it – either officially or (perhaps better) unofficially. The reason is that what you are doing is different; you are building a team, applying quality to your output, starting a cell of excellence. If you have a new name associated with that change, then these benefits will also be called to mind whenever the team is mentioned. Thus you establish advertising by association – although initially it will seem like just a bit of fun ('oh look, they've got a new name!'). To establish a new name, simply start using it: when answering the phone, signing a letter, sending a memo.

---

† *The Economist - 11th April 1992 - page 89*

Another aspect of marketing your team is to see what you can do for your internal customers. Look for opportunities to make friends with other groups by providing something they need but never hoped to get. If your team helps them with their work, these groups can only support your new ideas.

Another way to gain recognition is to promote the members of your team throughout the company. If there is a reward scheme in place, use it and publicize each success. As another example, one software team called their new program 'MAD' which stood for Michel, Alan and Daniel, the three main writers. Their leader then refused flatly to change the name before it was released to the world (who are told that MAD stands for Mixed Analog/Digital). On the one hand, it was a bit of fun; on the other hand, it gained that group an identity and inexorably linked their names with that software. Of course, if other people in your company have read this book these ideas will be recognized. So, either make contact when you recognize them – or be creative and think of new approaches, which is part of the fun.

11.3 Vision

One of the most cited characteristics of successful managers is that of vision. Of all the concepts in modern management, this is the one about which the most has been written. Of course different writers use it in different ways. One usage brings it to mean clairvoyance as in: 'she had great vision in foreseeing the demise of that market'. This meaning is of no use to you since crystal balls are only validated by hindsight and this book is concerned with your future.

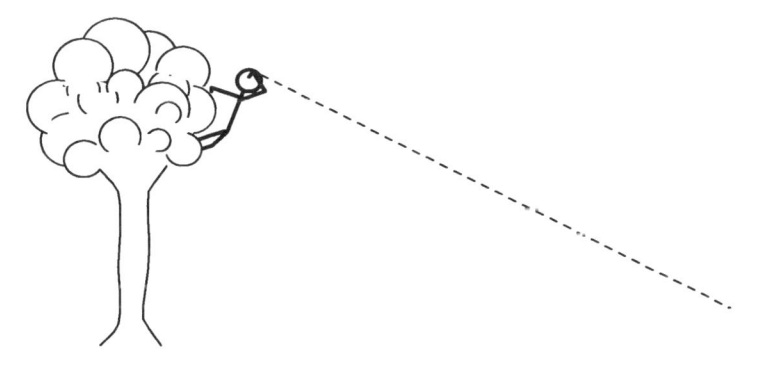

There is one meaning of vision which concerns you as a manager: a vivid idea of what the future should be. This has nothing to do with prediction but everything to do with hope. It is a focus for the team's activity, which provides sustained long-term motivation and which unites your team.

A vision has to be something sufficiently exciting to bind your team with you in common purpose. This implies two things:

- you need to decide where your team is headed
- you have to communicate that vision to them

Communicating a vision is not simply a case of painting it in large red letters across your office wall (although, as a stunt, this actually might be quite effective), but rather it is bringing the whole team to perceive your vision and to begin to share it with you. A vision, to be worthy, must become a guiding principle for the decisions and actions of your group.

Now, this vision thing, it is still a rather nebulous concept, hard to pin down, hard to define usefully; a vision may even be impractical (like 'zero defects'). And so there is an extra stage which assists in its communication: once you have identified your vision, you can illustrate it with a concrete goal, a *mission*. This leads to the creation of the famous 'mission statement'. Let us consider first what is a mission, and then return to the vision.

A mission has two important qualities:

- it should be tough, but achievable given sufficient effort
- it must be possible to tell when it has been achieved

To maintain an impetus, it might also have a time limit so that people can pace their activity rather than get winded in the initial push. The time limit on your mission statement, and the scope of your vision, will depend upon how high you have risen in the management structure. Heads of multinational corporations must take a longer view of the future than the project leader in divisional recruitment; the former may be looking at a strategy for the next twenty-five years, the latter may be concerned with attracting the current crop of senior school children for employment in two-three years. You, as a new manager, will want a mission which can be achieved within one or two years.

If you are stuck for a mission, think about using Quality as a focus since this is something on which you can build. Similarly, any aspects of *great* management which are not habitual in your team at the moment could be exemplified in a mission statement. For instance, if your team is involved in product design, your mission might be fully to automate the test procedures by the next product release; or more generally, your team mission might be to reduce by half the time spent in meetings within six months.

Once you have established a few possible mission statements, you can try to communicate (or decide upon) your *vision*. This articulates your underlying philosophy, your reasons for wanting the outcomes you have chosen. Not, please note, the ones you think you *should* choose but an honest statement of personal motivation; for it is only the latter which you will follow with conviction and which will convince others to follow you. In general, your vision should have no time limit, and be inspirational; it is the driving force which continues even when the mission statements have been achieved. Even so, it can be quite simple: Walt Disney's vision was 'to make people happy'. As a manager, yours might be something a little closer to your own team: mine is 'to make working here fun'.

There is no real call to make a public announcement of your vision or to place it on the notice board. Such affairs are quite common now, and normally attract mirth and disdain. If your vision is not communicated to your team by what you say and do, then you are not applying it yourself. It is *your* driving motivation. Once you have identified your vision, act on it with every decision you take.

11.4 Prescience

Genius is one per cent inspiration and ninety-nine percent perspiration (Thomas Edison)

Prescience is something for which you really have to work. Prescience is having foreknowledge of the future. Particularly as a Protector, you have to know in advance the events which impact upon your team. This may seem a little difficult at first but you will soon get the hang of it, particularly if you are playing *Watch the Manager*.

The key is *information* and there are three types:

- information you hear (tit-bits about travel, meetings, etc)
- information you gather (minutes of meetings, financial figure, etc)
- information you infer (*if* this happens *then* my team will need ...)

Information is absolutely vital. Surveys of decision-making in companies reveal that rapid and decisive decisions normally stem not from intuitive and extraordinary leadership but rather from the existence of an established information system covering the relevant data. Managers who know the full information can quickly reach an informed decision.

As a new manager, the influences upon you and your team stem mostly from within the company and this is where you must establish an active interest. Let us put that another way: if you do not keep your eyes open you are failing in your role as Protector to your team. Thus if your manager comes back from an important meeting, sit down with him/her afterwards and have a chat. There is no need to employ subterfuge, merely ask questions. If there are answers, you hear them; if there are none, you know to investigate elsewhere. If you can provide your manager with suggestions/ideas then you will benefit from his/her gratitude and future confidence(s). You should also talk to people in other departments; and never forget the secretaries who are normally the first to know everything.

Now some people love this aspect of the job, it makes them feel like politicians or espionage agents; others hate it, for exactly the same reasons. The point is that it must be done or you will be unprepared; but do not let it become a obsession.

Gathering information is not enough on its own: you have to process it and be aware of implications. The trick is to try to predict the next logical step from any changes you see. This can get very complicated, so try to restrict yourself to guessing one step at a time. Thus if the sales figures show a tailing off for the current product (and there are mutterings about the competition), then if you are in development, you might expect to be pressured for tighter schedules; if you are in publicity, there may soon be a request for launch material; if you are in sales, you might be asked to establish potential demand and practical pricing levels. Since you know this, you can have the information ready (or a reason not to comply) when it is first requested, and you and your team will shine.

Another way of generating information is to play '*what if*' games. If there is no obvious outcome to the current situation, imagine changes that might happen (or be made to happen) and see what effect these have on your team's future. There are dreadfully scientific ways of performing this sort of analysis, but reasonably you do not have the time. The sort of work this book is suggesting is that you, with your team or other managers (or both), play '*what if*' over coffee now and then. All you have to do is to postulate a novel question and see how it runs.

A very productive variation is to ask: 'what can go wrong?' By deliberately trying to identify potential problems at the onset, you will prevent many and compensate for many more.

Finally, set aside specific time to do this type of thinking. Call it *contingency planning* and put it in your diary as a regular appointment.

11.5 Changes of Focus

Without detracting from the main work, you can stimulate your team with changes of focus. This includes the drives for specific quality improvements (chapter 7), mission statements, team building activities (chapter 3), delegated authority (chapter 6), and so on. You have to decide how often to 'raise excitement' about new issues. On the one hand, too many focuses may distract or prevent the attainment of any one; on the other hand, changes in focus keep it fresh and maintain the excitement.

By practising this philosophy yourself, you also stimulate fresh ideas from your team because they see that it is a normal part of team practice to adopt and experiment with innovation. Thus not only are you relieved of the task of generating the new ideas, but also the individuals in your team acquire ownership in the whole creative process.

The really good news is that even a lousy choice of focus can have a beneficial effect. The most famous experiments in management studies were conducted between 1927 and 1932 by Elton Mayo and others at the Hawthorne works of the Western Electric Company in Chicago. The study was originally motivated by a failed experiment to determine the effect of lighting conditions on the production rates of factory workers. This experiment 'failed' because when the lighting conditions were changed for the experimental group, production *also* increased in the control group where no changes had been made. Essentially, Mayo took a small group of workers and varied different conditions (number and duration of breaks, shorter hours, refreshments, etc) to see how these actually affected production. The problem was not that production was unaffected but rather that whatever Mayo did, production increased – even when conditions were returned to their original state, production increased.

After many one-to-one interviews, Mayo deduced that the principal effect of his investigations had been to establish a team spirit amongst the group of workers. The girls [sic] who had formally worked in large groups were now a small team, they were consulted on the experiments, and the researchers displayed a keen interest in the way the girls were working and feeling about their work. Thus their own involvement and the interest shown in them were the reasons for the girls' increased productivity.

By providing changes of focus you build and motivate your team. For if you show in these changes that you are actively working to help them work, then they will feel that their efforts are recognized. If you also include their ideas in the changes, then they will feel themselves to be each a valued part of the team. If you pace these changes correctly, you can stimulate 'multiple Hawthorne effects' and continually increase productivity. And notice, this is not slave driving. The increased productivity of a Hawthorne effect comes from the enthusiasm of the workforce: they actually want to work better.

11.6 Flexibility

One of the main challenges in management is avoiding pat answers to everyday questions. There is nothing so dull, for you and your team, as your pulling out the same answer to every situation. It is also wrong. Each situation, and each person, is unique and no text-book answer will be able to embrace that uniqueness – except one: you are the manager, you have to judge each situation with a fresh eye, and you have to create the response. Your common sense and experience are your best guides in analysing the problem and in evolving your response.

Even if the established response seems suitable, you might still try something different. This is simple Darwinism. By trying variations upon standard models, you evolve new and potentially fitter models. If they do not work, you do not repeat them (although they might be tried in other circumstances); if they work better, then you have adapted and evolved.

This deliberate flexibility is not just an academic exercise to find the best answer. The point is that the situation and the environment are continually changing, and the rate of change is generally increasing with advancing technology. If you do not continually adapt (through experimentation) to accommodate these changes, then the solution which used to work (and which you still habitually apply) will no longer be appropriate. You will become the dodo. A lack of flexibility will cause stagnation and inertia. Not only do you not adapt, but the whole excitement of your work and your team diminishes as fresh ideas are lacking or lost.

Flexibility is also a necessary quantity when reviewing a plan (chapter 1). Since all plans are decided on the (limited) information which is available, you step off boldly as far as you dare. When you have gone that far, you review what information you have about the past and the projected future, and strike forth again. If the path disappears in front of you, you must be flexible enough to change direction or you will be lost forever and forever.

You can enhance your flexibility by increasing your experience and hence your options. This can be done either by deliberate learning on your part, or by involving others in formulating your decisions. Obviously, both approaches should be combined for best effect. Having got to this chapter, you have already decided to use reading as a source of learning (and you should continue) – however, observation of others is something you can do all the time, and talking with others will provide you with some of their learning also.

To encourage flexibility in your team, you should similarly encourage their learning and pooling of experience. Apart from training in specific skills and team building (chapter 3), you can also enhance flexibility specifically. For instance, you could challenge them with short unusual tasks (properly structured to include periods of review) or simply by job-swapping within the team. The latter has so many beneficial side-effects: reduced vulnerability to illness of one team member, increased understanding of other members' tasks, conversation and cooperation. Another approach is actively to encourage experimentation. If staff have a good idea, make time to explore it. Not only will this encourage them to innovate solutions as problems emerge, but it will also train them to take a flexible attitude to change since they will have initiated it themselves.

11.7 The Leaders

The basic problem with the style of leadership advocated in this book is that nearly every historic 'Leader' one can name has had a completely different approach. Machiavelli did not advocate team building and communication as the means of becoming a great leader but rather that a Prince ought to be happy with 'a reputation for being cruel in order to keep his subjects unified and loyal'. Your situation, however, is a little different. You do not have the power to execute, nor even to banish. The workforce is rapidly gaining in sophistication as the world grows more complex. You cannot effectively control through fear, so you must try another route. You could possibly gain compliance and rule your team through edict; but you would lose their input and experience, and gain only the burdens of greater decision making. You do not have the right environment to be a despot; you gain advantage by being a team leader.

A common mistake about the image of a leader is that you must be charismatic; that to lead, you need to be loud, flamboyant, and a great drinker or golfer or racket player or a great socialite to draw people to you. This is wrong. In any company, if you look hard enough, you will find quiet modest people who lead teams with great success and personal satisfaction. If you are quiet and modest, fear not; all you need is to talk clearly to the people who matter (your team) and they will hear you.

So what makes a great leader?

The leaders are the ones who challenge the existing complacency and who are prepared to lead their team forward towards a personal vision. They are the ones who recognize problems, seize opportunities, and create their own future. Ultimately, they are the ones who stop to think where they want to go and then have the shameless audacity to set out.

You have the power – using your own common sense.